HOW TO SURVIVE A FREAKIN' NUCLEAR WAR

A CRASH COURSE ON SURVIVING NUCLEAR WAR AND GUERILLA WARFARE

BILL O'NEILL

ISBN: 978-1-64845-113-3

DON'T FORGET YOUR FREE BOOK

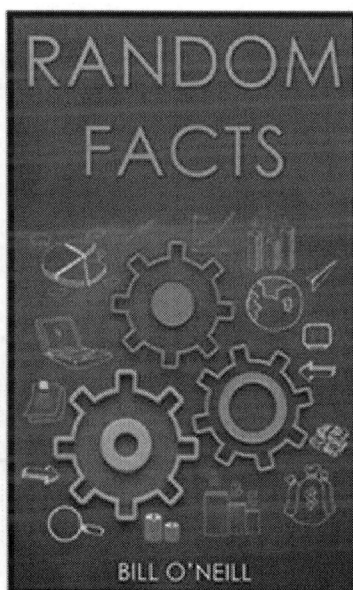

GET THEM FOR FREE ON
WWW.TRIVIABILL.COM

CONTENTS

DISCLAIMER

This book is primarily intended for entertainment and popular interest purposes only. Although every effort has been made to ensure the advice and guidelines presented in this book are accurate, these explanations are light-hearted and cursory, and should not replace the formal advice and instructions of survival experts and those with professional experience in the subjects and situations discussed here. The advice and lifehacks that follow should not be attempted without further research and without taking on board the specialist knowledge of genuine experts in these fields. This is a book intended to help you stay safe - so always prioritize your own safety!

INTRODUCTION

When disaster strikes, there will always be two kinds of people: those who are prepared, and those who aren't. The former stand to succeed in the face of adversity, while the latter are doomed to crumble into dust when confronted with even the smallest hiccup.

That's why we've put this series of books together to help teach you the basic principles of how to keep yourself and your loved ones alive in extreme, life-threatening circumstances. We can reflect on the words of the great Benjamin Franklin to help us understand the gravity of preparation, "by failing to prepare, you are preparing to fail, now get me a blanket."

In *How to Survive a Freakin' Bear Attack* we covered the basic survival skills and hacks you should employ to prepare for and survive the aftermath of a bear attack. In this book, we're going to do the same thing, only this time, we'll be covering the specifics of how to survive a nuclear war.

A nuclear war is one of the most cataclysmic disasters that you should prepare for. While many people are familiar with nuclear explosions based on what they have seen in movies or read in history books, far fewer truly understand the immense devastation a nuclear war would inflict upon the world and the severe consequences it would leave behind in its wake. A single nuclear bomb will kill millions of people in an instant, but an all-out nuclear war could result in hundreds of millions (if not billions) of fatalities all over the world.

Within seconds, a nuclear explosion would decimate an entire city. The blast would send out a shockwave of immense heat traveling like a firestorm hundreds of miles an hour, toppling buildings, causing mass fires, inflicting severe burns, and disrupting the TV schedules for the foreseeable future. Over the long term, the fallout from a detonated nuclear weapon would contaminate the environment, resulting in radiation sickness for millions of people over the upcoming decades. The ash sent up into the sky would block out the sun, causing a nuclear winter and throwing the entire world into darkness and famine. But hey-ho, at least traffic won't be an issue anymore!

Your chances of surviving this may seem remote..., but it is certainly possible and that's why learning how to prepare for a nuclear fallout is so important. Why resign yourself to certain death, when you can learn to stay alive like the Bee Gees in this society of possibility and (probably) mutated rats. It's all in the preparation.

In this book, we'll cover the most important survival skills and hacks to help you prepare for a nuclear war, survive the initial blast, and stay alive in a new world completely reshaped by the fallout of nuclear weapons.

We'll cover the horrors of what a nuclear war would look like and the long-term effects of a nuclear blast, how to build a nuclear shelter, and the most important items to stockpile in preparation for a nuclear blast. Before then diving into what you need to do when you know a nuclear attack is imminent and how to react in the immediate aftermath of the nuclear explosion.

We'll also cover how to keep yourself sanitized from nuclear radiation and how to treat yourself or a loved one when exposed, how to find provisions, tips on keeping yourself safe, and the importance of building a community so you can band together with like-minded people to help ensure your survival.

The goal of this book is not to scare you but rather to give you hope. After reading this book, you will not only understand just how devastating a nuclear war would be, but you will also learn how surviving a nuclear war is possible and the steps you can take to protect yourself and those you love. You may also take the time to figure out how to bake your own bread, because no-one will be doing that for you.

CHAPTER ONE:

WHAT WOULD A NUCLEAR WAR LOOK LIKE?

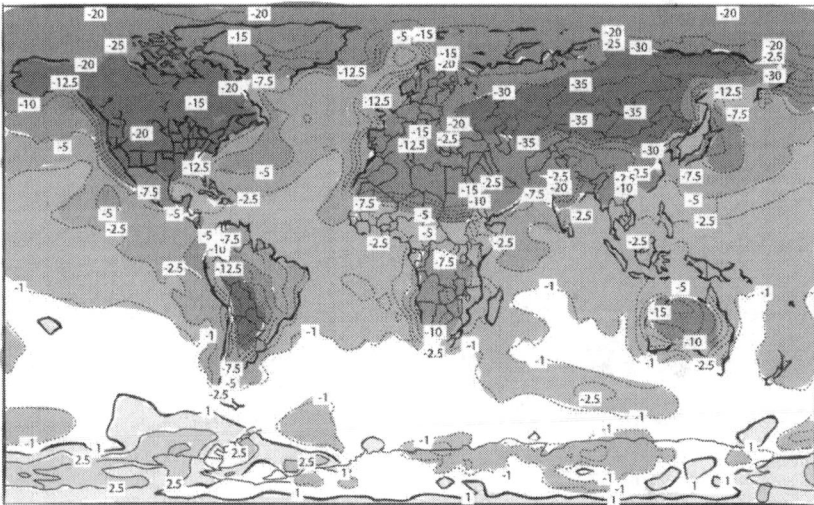

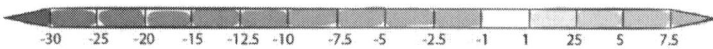

Let's be realistic here, a nuclear war would be an unprecedented human disaster that would completely reshape the way we live. Nuclear apocalypse would be the most disruptive event since the T-Rex looked into the sky and muttered "that rock looks like it's getting mighty close". While an economic collapse, natural disaster, or political or societal unrest may seem more likely to occur than a nuclear war, none of those three would be as catastrophic.

An economic collapse would eventually result in an economic recovery, a natural disaster would be devastating but localized, and civil unrest would eventually dissipate or be put down by the authorities. All three would be devastating in the short term but would either not affect the world on a global scale or be recoverable in a few months or years.

Nuclear war is different because it would result in death and destruction on a global scale to a degree unlike anything we had ever seen, and in ways no other disaster would be able to inflict. The way you would live afterwards (if you survived) would be completely different from the way you live now.

The possibility of a nuclear war was seen as a major threat during the Cold War, especially during the Cuban Missile Crisis in 1962. In the aftermath of the Cold War, however, the world witnessed the proliferation of nuclear weapons and the potential for catastrophic conflict has not gone away. Today, nine nuclear states possess more than 13,000 nuclear warheads, including nuclear missiles, with the United States and Russia holding the vast majority of these nuclear arsenals, like two grumpy siblings who won't share their radioactive candy. The fact is that several nuclear weapons exist, and their destructive power is immense. The UK's Trident submarines, for instance, each carry an explosive force greater than the total that was used in Hiroshima and Nagasaki in World War II.

Understanding the different nuclear war scenarios and types of nuclear weapons is crucial to grasping the devastating consequences that would happen as a result of a nuclear war.

There are two primary kinds of nuclear weapons: tactical and strategic. Tactical nuclear weapons are intended for use on the battlefield to obliterate enemy combatants and units, while strategic nuclear weapons are used to target cities and urban areas (like the atomic bomb blasts at Hiroshima and Nagasaki), designed to wipe out civilians and infrastructure. As a civilian yourself, strategic nuclear weapons are far more likely to be a threat to you.

The atomic bombs dropped on Hiroshima and Nagasaki in 1945 demonstrated the horrifying consequences of strategic nuclear weapons, killing over 200,000 people and leaving survivors with long-term health problems due to radiation exposure. Hundreds of thousands of people died of radiation exposure and sickness in the years after the bombings.

****

Full-scale nuclear war would involve the use of thousands of nuclear warheads, with both strategic and tactical nuclear weapons likely to be used. The immediate effects of a nuclear explosion include radiation and heat, blast and shock waves, as well as radioactive fallout. In the event of a nuclear attack, these consequences would be devastating. And that's only the start.

A single strategic nuclear explosion going off in your city would result in widespread destruction of the surrounding area and hundreds of thousands of fatalities. The incredible heat generated from the explosion would incinerate anyone within its radius, while the blast shockwaves would knock down even the strongest of buildings in your city to the ground and reduce them to a pile of charred rubble.

This is because a fireball of superheated air is generated within microseconds of a nuclear weapon going off. Energy will be released in the form of X-rays, which creates intense heat that immediately causes temperatures to soar within the immediate environment. This energy will manifest in the form of lethal levels of gamma rays and neutrons. Depending on the type of weapon used, the zone of lethal radiation can extend up to or over a mile in all directions from the immediate fatalities.

Anyone within that zone would be incinerated or burned to death almost immediately, while anyone else close by would end with severe burns that they would carry with them for the rest of their lives. To give you a perspective, in the event of a 300-kiloton nuclear weapon going off, the resulting heat can inflict first-degree burns on victims up to more than eight miles away. The blast will initially travel faster than the speed of sound as well, so attempting to drive away in a car from the blast if you're within approximately eight miles won't do you any good.

Furthermore, when a nuclear blast goes off it will set off an electromagnetic pulse, otherwise known as an EMP. An EMP has a very similar effect to a solar flare from the sun that reaches Earth. It produces a very intense pulse of electromagnetic energy that will short-circuit virtually all electronic equipment within the radius of the blast. In an instance, the power will go completely out, the water will stop running, laptops and tablets and phones will cease to work, there will be no more internet or cell service, and most vehicles will cease working as well.

****

In short, a nuclear blast would immediately and literally throw cities back to the Stone Ages, although not in the same way Fred Flintstone knows it. Those lucky enough to survive the blast will find themselves in a city reduced to rubble, with no power, internet or cell service, and with most people suffering from radiation sickness and severe burns. As the hours, days, weeks, and months roll on, more and more people will be affected by the fallout leading to a rising death toll and casualties.

And this is only on a localized scale, the global consequences of a worldwide nuclear war would be even more catastrophic. Not only would the same city-level blasts, sickness, radiation, and so on happen on a global scale, the world would witness an incoming nuclear winter, disruption of food production, and societal collapse.

Nuclear winter is a phenomenon that results in a prolonged cooling of the Earth's surface due to the injection of soot into the atmosphere that will partially block out the sun. This shoot will result from massive fires caused by nuclear explosions. The potential ramifications of a nuclear winter include extensive cooling of the Earth's surface, a complete collapse of the global agricultural system, and a near-complete halt to food production.

This will then result in worldwide famine, and starvation will result for the survivors who are lucky enough to survive the initial explosions. Existing stores of food would be quickly consumed, forcing people to scavenge for food or attempt to grow their own, which would be immensely difficult in most areas due to the ash in the air. In short, a worldwide nuclear war would result in a global food crisis completely unmatched in history.

In short, a nuclear war would completely change the way survivors live and would be felt for generations. The impacts would have devastating consequences for the world and all of us living within it, but that doesn't mean that survival even over the long term will be impossible.

But even though a nuclear war would easily be the most devastating disaster that could ever affect the planet (short of an extinction-level event from an asteroid or a major plague), through it all, survival will be possible. After all, that's why you're reading this book!

Later in this book, we'll dive deep into the most important tips you can follow to survive the aftermath of a nuclear war. First, let's look more closely at how the world will have changed in the weeks, months, and years after a nuclear war has struck.

CHAPTER TWO:

WHAT WOULD THE WORLD LOOK LIKE AFTER A NUCLEAR WAR HAS HAPPENED?

At this point, you might very well be sitting there and thinking "this whole nuclear apocalypse business isn't anywhere near as fun as I thought it'd be!" And you'd be right. However, you can only survive such an event if you know what you're up against. This book might be a little bit grizzly at times, but you'll be laughing when drinking an out-of-date soda in your bunker while your neighbor has just finished growing their seventh eye. They won't laugh at you for buying this book then, will they? Take that Gerald!

You may say, "a nuclear war would never happen," but keep in mind that nine countries each possess thousands of nuclear weapons and are individually capable of causing the immeasurable devastation as described in Chapter One. With ever-rising geopolitical tensions around the world as well, it's not hard to imagine that a future nuclear conflict could be a very real scenario. Though of course, we all hope it doesn't happen, and the creators of this book would like to implore any and all nation leaders across the planet to **not press the red button**, and to make it very clear that this book is no endorsement of nuclear warfare.

While we've glossed over some vague details, this chapter will explore what a post-nuclear war world looks like. We'll investigate the devastating effects that could result from these nine nuclear states engaging each other in conflict well as the immediate aftermaths following an engagement between two or more nations armed with nuclear weapons.

****

In the aftermath of a nuclear explosion, life on Earth would descend into chaos. The immense strength of each blast would demolish cities and obliterate infrastructure in seconds. An untold number of people would be immediately killed, with many more injured. For the next several decades following a nuclear war, hundreds of thousands of people (if not millions) would continue to slowly die each year due to succumbing to radiation exposure. A post-nuclear war world would perhaps be the single greatest catalyst for a human extinction-level event short of a severe and irreversible global pandemic or an asteroid hitting the Earth.

Accompanying the massive levels of destruction, entire global political and national ecosystems would cease to exist, and bands of survivors would attempt to gain power and control over resources for themselves. This is something that is unpredictable, and we can't understand what would really happen. If TV shows like *The Walking Dead* are anything to go by, entire towns of survivors would emerge with an insidious agenda. Cannibalism could become rife and those who survive might be hunted for sport or for food as supplies dwindle. However, it's just as plausible that peaceful communes are founded, that focus on the growth of crops and management of livestock. Removed from the stresses of modernity and all societal structure, some may settle into a Hobbit-style existence, living slowly and having hairy feet.

The biggest threat once all the bombs have fallen will be radiation poisoning. It will kill some people instantly and others slowly over months or years depending on the amount of radiation a person is exposed to. In the 40 years from 1945 to 1985, experts estimated that millions of people who survived the blasts at Hiroshima and Nagasaki died in the years afterwards from their bodies slowly succumbing to the radiation sickness in the atmosphere.

Firestorms would rage across cities and vast swaths of wilderness, sending continuing billows of ash into the sky. There would be limited or no emergency services available to combat the fires like there are in the case of wildfires because whatever the emergency response, medical, or law enforcement services are left would be focused on dealing with trying to help everyone, furthermore, many personnel in those positions would likely abandon their posts in a frantic attempt to find their families or for self-preservation.

It's also possible that regional conflicts will continue after a nuclear war. Even after Country A and Country B have decimated the other with nuclear weapons, for instance, they may still engage in armed conflict with one another in certain areas of the world depending on if still possess any degree of military strength.

A 2019 analysis of a limited nuclear engagement between India and Pakistan found just how devastating a nuclear war would be even on a nuclear scale. The analysis focused on a hypothetical war between India and Pakistan in which both countries used 100 15-kiloton devices directly against one another. The study found that nearly 30 million people across both nations would be killed nearly instantly. Now imagine that on a global scale.

Lastly, because of the EMP explosion that accompanies the blast, all communications, cell service, and internet services might be knocked out instantly. You're no longer able to get in touch with the outside world or understand what's happening, but little do you know, hundreds of nuclear explosions have likewise gone off all over the world. Short-wave radios might function, but long-distance communication may become lost for the foreseeable future. No phone calls, and worst of all there's no *Wikipedia*, so you can't even search 'nuclear apocalypse' (before becoming distracted and accidentally spending 3 hours browsing irrelevant pages about increasingly niche and boring topics) …

Now how will your life change?

****

Long story short, your life will change because every minute of every day will become about one thing: survival for yourself and survival of your loved ones. It's important to understand that nuclear war would go far beyond the destruction and casualties in the moment of explosion. enough. In time, a nuclear conflict could disrupt global climate patterns with potentially cataclysmic consequences for ecosystems. The aftermath of this

15

calamity would cause society to disintegrate. Governments would fail to maintain order, and millions of survivors would flee cities in an attempt to escape the radiation poisoning in the explosion cities while countless more are left behind to slowly die from the burns and radiation.

To say that the world would descend into chaos would be understating it. You'd be just as well off saying 'it's gone off the rails a bit'. The days of you going to work, checking social media, driving your car around, going to the homes of friends and family on a Saturday for a BBQ, watching movies at the theater, taking a winter vacation to somewhere tropical, going out to eat at restaurants, shopping at grocery stores, and having a relaxing evening at home with your dog while watching TV will all be a thing of the past. McDonalds may even have to close some of its sites.

Making money will no longer be a concern for you, however. Money won't matter at all in fact, at least not for a while. Instead, the new commodities will be food, water, and everyday items that we too often take for granted each day, such as personal hygiene or first aid items. In short, you'll no longer be able to enjoy the comforts that everyday life affords you now, and your life will no longer be about making money to pay the bills and saving up enough for retirement. Your entire life will become about scavenging for food and other essentials, protecting yourself from radiation exposure, protecting your stockpiles and your life from armed raiding parties, and finding a way to grow your own food in a nuclear winter.

Once upon a time this is how humanity existed, through trading. It's likely that sometime after 'the event', money would be re-instated, and commodities will once again be traded. But it's unlikely to happen in your (now shorter) lifetime.

The certainty of a 'nuclear winter' following a nuclear war is commonly overlooked. The prospect of nuclear winter, which will arise from the devastating fallout caused by a nuclear war or conflict, is deeply concerning. If an armed confrontation between India and Pakistan were to happen in the above hypothetical example, even on a limited scale, experts warned that catastrophic effects could occur worldwide. Beyond the 30 million people who would be instantly killed in those two countries, globally we might see drops in global ocean temperatures by as much as 38.3 degrees Fahrenheit. Doesn't matter how many North Face jackets you have at your disposal; it's going to get chilly.

Alteration of our planet's atmosphere leading to the start of another ice age is another possibility if the sun becomes blocked out by the ash clouds for a long enough time. Whether that would happen is entirely dependent on how severe a future nuclear war is and how much ash is sent into the sky. If enough ash is sent into the sky and blocks out the sun, darkness will envelop the Earth like a long-term solar eclipse, and temperatures would drop substantially to freezing levels.

Ecosystems would of course be severely damaged due to the extreme coldness and darkness that would ensue from smoke-filled skies blocking out sunlight, resulting after massive firestorms ignited through these explosions. Animals that survive will migrate to habitable areas or behave in new and bizarre ways in order to live in this newer, colder world.

The consequences of a nuclear winter would decimate food production, particularly in regard to agriculture. As temperatures dropped drastically worldwide, yields in mid-high latitude countries would take an immense hit. Food production would decrease by an estimated nearly 90% within three or four years after such a conflict broke out, meaning potentially billions would face famine due to lack of sustenance.

Severe agricultural failures and food shortages would cause an unprecedented breakdown in society if the blasts and resulting fallout don't cause that break down already. Governments wouldn't have enough resources to offer adequate services or keep order as their people suffer from hunger and desperation. This crisis would bring about massive migration as people look for safety and better opportunities, and what remains of governments will no longer be able to control the population.

Unfortunately, this movement would only deepen instability, generating conflict throughout affected regions and resulting in widespread anarchy. Groups of survivors would clash with each other for precious resources, resulting in groups forming their own 'tribes' and laying claim to the land.

In light of this, it is essential to explore how exactly such warfare might affect the environment in both short-term and long-term scenarios. The battle won't just be for food and water, but also to stay alive in a world that is nearly completely contaminated with life-threatening nuclear radiation. This includes contamination of land or water sources, which can have serious repercussions for biodiversity, not to mention making much food and water unsafe to consume.

Disruption of marine ecosystems as well as various other potentially damaging effects over an extended period would follow, meaning that attempting to find food from the oceans may not be viable either. The environmental impact that a nuclear war would have on ocean temperatures, and the arctic sea ice in particular, could be devastating. Marine ecosystems as well as fisheries that provide sustenance to billions around the world would suffer greatly if catches were depleted and fish populations decreased due to radiation contamination.

In essence, contaminated land and water sources would exacerbate food shortages as well as health issues for those exposed to the radiation. Even if you protect yourself from burns and nuclear radiation from the outside, if you consume contaminated food then you could physically destroy yourself from the inside. If you're starving and desperate for food, you might not think about the above either, meaning you won't give much thought to discerning which food is safe to eat and what isn't.

A nuclear war would lead to an irreparable loss of biodiversity and put Earth's ecosystems in immense danger. Whole habitats could be obliterated from ongoing fires left unchecked while many plant and animal species may never recover from such massive disruption. Even if humanity manages to survive a global nuclear conflict, countless species of plants and animal life will face absolute extinction, which would change the flora and fauna of the Earth in ways unseen since the end of the last Ice Age more than ten thousand years ago.

Ultimately, nuclear war will carry with it far-reaching ramifications that go beyond the destruction of lives and property. It will completely change ecosystems, natural habitats, and wilderness from one end of the globe to the other. The entire world will feel the consequences in one way or another, and life will never be the same again.

CHAPTER THREE:

WHAT WILL BE THE EFFECTS OF A NUCLEAR BLAST?

So far, we have primarily covered how the world will change as a result of a large-scale nuclear war. But now we need to ask ourselves an equally important question: what will be the immediate effects of a nuclear explosion?

The destruction caused by nuclear weapons is incomparable to any other force on the planet and can lead to devastating consequences in just a fraction of a second, destroying whole cities and claiming tens of millions of lives. Hopefully, you fully comprehend all of this at this point, and if you don't, re-read chapter two but make sure you stop a few times and say "wow" to really drill the point home.

Total number of deaths caused directly by a nuclear exchange between the US and Russia, in expectation

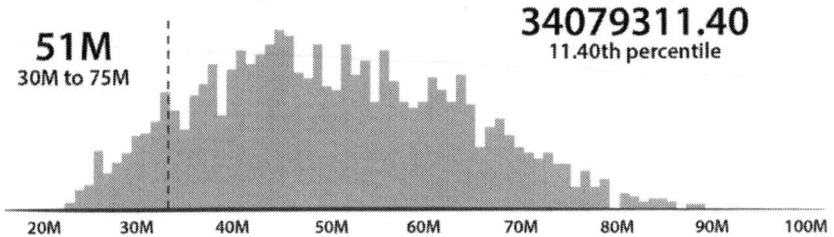

51M
30M to 75M

34079311.40
11.40th percentile

20M   30M   40M   50M   60M   70M   80M   90M   100M

To comprehend how a nuclear blast works, two major factors are responsible for such destruction: thermal radiation and blast waves coming from the detonation.

When we refer to the initial stages after a nuclear explosion that is followed by massive damage to buildings and infrastructure, these aforementioned factors each play their own role. While thermal radiation radiates outward at tremendous speed forming firestorms due to its extreme heat, so does the pressure created by the shock wave generated by high-intensity supersonic winds. The reverberations of these waves can reach and be felt many hundreds of miles away.

****

The detonation of a 1,000-kiloton nuclear bomb will be felt as follows: within seven miles of ground zero (the immediate site of the blast), individuals will either be vaporized into particles in thin air instantly or suffer first-degree burns. The burns will be so severe that anyone affected will either perish instantly or slowly die depending on where the burns are located. Imagine yourself in a home or building that is set completely ablaze and experiencing your whole body or parts of your body completely engulfed in flames before you manage to get out. If you are unable to imagine that, then imagine you have placed instantly into the middle of a freshly cooked McDonalds Apple Pie... now do you see what we're trying to say? If professional medical help weren't to arrive right away, you would die. The effects will be very similar if you're within a seven-mile radius of the blast and out in the open. Additionally, those fifty or more miles away will experience temporary blindness if they look directly at the blast, so it's important not to drive heavy machinery directly afterwards.

A nuclear blast will have permanent repercussions for people that go beyond physical harm as well. Those affected by the blast and lucky enough to survive over the long term could still suffer from post-traumatic stress disorder (PTSD), unease, or depression. This will cause massive problems with social order if many people are affected this way. Generations of people might be motivation-less, yearning for a tub of ice cream and the first 5 series of *Friends*. Except they won't be able to have either.

Extensive damage to structures as well as access to services would most likely lead to economic hardship resulting in massive relocations. People would migrate by the thousands to look for areas that are less contaminated or affected by the blast.

The shock wave triggered by a nuclear explosion is immensely powerful, causing widespread destruction near the epicenter and extending its reach dozens of miles beyond in all directions. Everything in the path of a nuclear shockwave will ensure significant devastation: buildings will collapse, vehicles will be crushed, and people and animals will be sent flying like rag dolls against the ground and buildings as if they were caught up in a tornado. Very little will be able to survive near the blast, save for cockroaches and the remaining members of the *Rolling Stones*, who will begin planning their 400th tour for later that same year.

But there's more to this blast wave than physical damage. A nuclear shockwave also carries deadly ionizing radiation, which can lead to cancer or genetic mutations from radiation sickness. This is a key theme to remember throughout this book. There will be two long-lasting ramifications that will greatly affect the way we live in a post-nuclear war environment: the nuclear winter that plunges the world into cold and darkness, and the radiation that can slowly eat away at our bodies from the inside out depending on how intensely we were affected.

This destructive power originates from an enormous amount of energy released during a detonation that covers all areas on the electromagnetic spectrum. This was made evident through testing these weapons, which showed scientists firsthand how devastating the effects of nuclear shockwaves were.

The destruction is primarily due to the intense heat energy, or thermal radiation, which is released during the blast. This scalding burst of radiant heat can vaporize anything around

24

ground zero and cause severe first-degree or second-degree burns on any exposed skin or flesh. It will spark fires over a wide range that eventually merge into one giant conflagration known as a firestorm, which will then be carried by wind and cover vast swathes of land. Pristine forests, prairies, and other wilderness areas will become completely engulfed in flames. The fires will start near the site of the explosion and gradually spread from there. As we covered in the last chapter, without emergency first responders, there will be nothing to keep these fires contained.

Such occurrences are especially worrying in modern urban environments where construction density often necessitates smaller distances between buildings than what was previously seen with Germany and Japan's safety zones established during World War II (which were about 30–50 feet). Considering all factors involved (from how powerful the nuclear weapon was to local atmospheric conditions) there's the potential for large-scale disasters caused not just directly by the initial bomb wave but also through its aftermath of flames everywhere else.

Understanding precisely the damage brought about by a nuclear explosion is key to recognizing the full ramifications of a nuclear explosion. Atmospheric nuclear tests conducted around the world have decisively proven that exposure to such radiation may lead not only to acute sickness but also long-term health issues, even damage at the genetic level. Even those who escape unharmed from a blast are still at risk of developing serious illnesses down the road due to this exposure. In other words, even if you're hundreds of miles away from the site of the nuclear blast, you're still at severe risk of becoming exposed to radiation and will need to take preventative measures accordingly.

****

It's important to note that you may believe the above will only happen on a large scale in the event of the worst-case scenario, such as all countries who possess nuclear weapons releasing their nuclear bombs at each other at once. In reality, utilizing less than 1% of the world's nuclear armaments would be more than enough to throw the global climate off balance. Experts have estimated that if only 1% of the world's nuclear bombs are released, the lives of up to two billion people after the explosions themselves could be lost through starvation caused by the ensuing famine that is brought about in part by heightened levels of radioactive fallout.

When it comes to the long-term effects of a nuclear explosion, radioactive fallout poses an ongoing risk for environmental contamination. As we briefly explored in the last chapter, food and water sources initially untouched by the blast can still become highly contaminated and unsafe to eat. You can become contaminated with radiation even if you are far away from the site of the initial blast.

Radioactive fallout means that physical, chemical, biological, and radiological substances can accumulate in the air, water, and soil around us, inflicting a severe impact on ecosystems as well as human health. Radioactive material can also be absorbed into our bodies if left unchecked over extended periods, causing harm down the line.

Taking action to mitigate any harmful side-effects from environmental contamination resulting from radioactive fallout is paramount. If any authorities or emergency first responders are still present and taking action, hazardous materials used along with appropriate disposal techniques will need to be implemented alongside careful monitoring of any areas that are impacted by radioactivity levels. In addition to these proactive prevention methods, however, emergency response protocols must be highly responsive to contain and clean up contaminated zones while providing medical aid to those affected at the same time.

If none of the above is possible after a nuclear explosion due to the obliteration of emergency first response teams or their ability to respond, then the sole responsibility of protecting yourself from radiation after an explosion will fall on one person: you.

It goes without saying how important safety measures are when dealing with scenarios involving nuclear weapons. Such steps will not only provide protection now but ensure future generations' lives remain safe going forward regardless of whether there is ever another nuclear blast or not. Cleaning up radioactive material is a little more complicated than using cloth and soap, nor should you employ the use of oven mitts. Later in this book, we'll discuss preventative measures you can take to protect yourself from nuclear radiation immediately after a blast as well as over the long term.

****

Earlier in this book, we made mention of how a nuclear blast will trigger a very powerful electromagnetic pulse (EMP) that disrupts electronic devices, communication networks, and satellites. In our modern world, this will cause chaos. We rely heavily on technology for regular functioning and communication with other people we know, unless you live in Southern France. Without electricity, internet access, or reliable transportation systems, life as we know it would be severely impaired. A full-scale nuclear war could undo hundreds of years of technological advancement.

The United States government has preventative measures in place in the event an enemy force was to detonate an EMP device in the atmosphere high enough that it causes the power grid to collapse from one coast to the other. But these measures do not include handling an EMP attack in addition to a nuclear strike (or multiple nuclear strikes), nor does it account for this happening on a global level.

Imagine a world where the power grid, internet, cell service, technological devices, and most vehicles completely cease working instantly literally everywhere in addition to a nuclear winter setting in and radiation sweeping through the air we breathe. Your ability to breathe and see clearly will be hindered, and your senses completely overwhelmed. It'll be like living in a *Lush* store 24/7, but with fewer assistants asking you how your day has been. This will be the very real world we would live in if nuclear war breaks out.

Apart from the above destruction caused by radiation exposure and fallout following detonation, there are also threats posed by the significant pulses created out of energy thrown off during the explosion. These include personal everyday computers and tablets being affected along with military communications reconnaissance equipment being vulnerable to compromise, among other things. This could lead to dangerous predicaments should precautions not be taken into consideration adequately beforehand.

Last but not least, the destructive power of a nuclear blast would not just result in physical destruction but would also take an emotional toll on those affected. Long-lasting psychological impacts could include PTSD, anxiety, depression, and survivor guilt, as well as increased suicide rates. The deep trauma experienced by survivors may cause social disorder resulting from infrastructure disruption and population displacement; all these factors would combine to create immense distress for individuals within the community at large. Even long after a detonation has occurred, people may no longer possess the willpower or the mental strength to survive.

****

So, what can you do? Taking preventative steps and having an emergency plan in place ahead of time will help minimize destruction if a nuclear strike was to occur in your area. Being aware of the risks associated with a nuclear detonation and ensuring everyone has plans for how they would react could save lives when disaster strikes. It is essential for people involved in any kind of potential threat posed by this type of blast to understand what needs to happen immediately, and before much damage occurs due to their actions or lack thereof.

Knowing how to protect yourself during and after a nuclear explosion is also important. Being aware of the potential risks associated with such events, like thermal radiation, radioactive fallout, blast wave effects, and EMP disruptions, can help individuals stay safe before or after an event. A sound emergency plan should also be established ahead of time that covers appropriate actions for each stage: sheltering in place if possible, evacuating safely from danger zones, as well as decontamination steps once it's over. Taking these precautionary measures helps people take control of their safety so they don't suffer undue damage following a nuclear detonation.

The consequences of a nuclear blast are immense and can have long-term repercussions in all aspects of our lives. From the destruction at ground zero to potentially hazardous radiation, we must take preventative steps toward safeguarding ourselves from such an event. By being proactive with knowledge of the risks posed by a nuclear explosion and ways to protect communities, together we can create a safe future for everyone.

Additionally, make sure that you are continuously informed about potential dangers associated with this level of destruction if catastrophe strikes, ranging from physical harm caused by blasts or fallout damage that could affect people's homes as well as psychological stress-related incidents so that adequate action may be taken before any serious threats arise. Now more than ever, prevention plays its part. Let's work together today to ensure safer days ahead.

By this point in this book, we have clearly established just how devastating a single nuclear blast would be, let alone multiple blasts.

In short, the destructive power of a nuclear war will cause:

- Entire buildings are to be reduced to rubble within the seven-mile radius of a blast.
- People will sustain thermal and first-degree burns on exposed skin, and air-blast-related injuries such as collapsed buildings and projectile debris.
- Eye damage including temporary blindness due to retinal burns, as well as radiation poisoning (otherwise known medically as acute radiation syndrome or ARS). The latter is a devastating illness marked by vomiting, diarrhea, and hair loss along with other potentially lethal symptoms.
- Wildfires spread across prairies, forests, and mountains, sending incalculable amounts of ash into the sky to block out the sun.

- The resulting electromagnetic pulse will completely knock down the power grid and shut off electrical devices, running water, and most vehicles, sending the world back to the Stone Ages almost quite literally.
- Food and water sources will become contaminated by radiation, meaning that people can become poisoned with radiation and slowly die from the inside out.
- Many people will become utterly shocked, depressed, and suicidal as many will lose the will to try to survive.
- A sharp rise in the price of firewood and forks.

CHAPTER FOUR:

AVOIDING THE SITE
OF A NUCLEAR BLAST

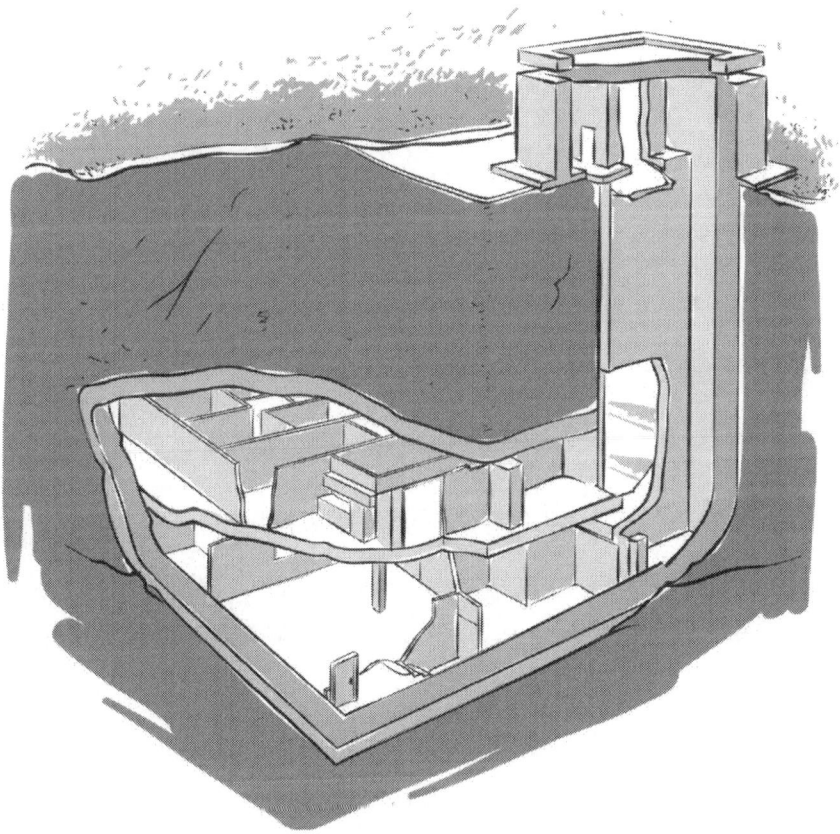

The easiest way to avoid the immediate effects of a nuclear blast is to get away from it. This should be simple, no fire drill has ever started with "upon discovery of an uncontrolled blaze in the building, place your head within 2 inches of the flame and inhale sharply, before placing both hands into the epicenter." It is best to be as far away from the blast as possible.

Today, hypersonic nuclear missiles are capable of traveling more than four thousand miles per hour, meaning that it will only require each missile mere minutes to cross the Pacific or Atlantic oceans to reach their intended targets. In other words, if you're within the general target site, you're simply not going to get away in time even if you have forewarning of the nuclear strike.

Ideally, you'll want to be at least one hundred miles away from the nearest blast site. This won't make you totally invulnerable nor will it guarantee your survival in general because you'll have to contend with a collapse of the national power grid from the EMP that comes with the nuclear explosion, the halt to supply chains, and the complete breakdown of society, among other things. However, you probably won't immediately die, which most people would agree is a good thing.

Staying as far away from possible from the site of a nuclear blast will be to your advantage for three big (and hopefully obvious) reasons:

1. You will be away from the extreme heat that will be generated from the explosive power of the blast, and thus will avoid being served well-done to the rats of the city.

2. You will be away from any major population sources (hopefully), and thus avoid the ensuring chaos following an explosion or being exposed out in the open to looters and raiding parties.

3. Perhaps most importantly, the chances of you being vaporized or infected with radiation immediately following the blast by being far enough outside of the blast zone.

So how can you avoid the site of a nuclear blast before it happens?

Avoiding Nuclear Hotspots

The key is to stay away from what is called a nuclear 'hotspot', which is a site that would be likely targeted by enemy forces armed with nuclear weapons. If you live in a village where there's one shop, you know most people by name, and you don't have to lock your door in the day - you're probably not living in a nuclear hotspot.

However, in the United States alone, there are numerous hotspots all over the country from coast-to-coast that would likely be targeted in the event of a nuclear war. Thinking that living a hundred miles away from the site of a big city will make you safe is a major overlook. You need to stay at least a hundred miles away from any nuclear hotspot, and while major cities and population centers are indeed hotspots, they will also not be the only hotspots in the event of a nuclear war. The same concept goes for any other country and not just the United States, but we'll use the USA as an example, because Americans don't know where any other country is.

You'll recall that there are two primary types of nuclear weapons:

- Strategic nuclear weapons, which are used against urban sites and meant to eliminate vast swaths of the population and general infrastructure.
- Tactical nuclear weapons, which are meant to eliminate enemy combat forces, military bases, and military countermeasures such as missile sites.

Both types could be deployed in the event of a nuclear war.

In the United States, strategic nuclear weapons would be deployed against the big cities, including the cities mentioned above. Tactical nuclear weapons, however, would be launched against military installations and nuclear power plants all over the country in an attempt to severely cripple (if not outright dismantle) the country's defenses, nuclear power, and ability to launch counter strikes. In America, there are many military bases and nuclear power plants dotted all over the country, and each of every one of them will be a potential hotspot in a nuclear war. You'll want to make sure that you're away from these hotspots when the blast goes off in addition to being away from the big cities, because they will be a likely target.

The United States currently possesses over ninety active nuclear power reactors throughout the country, each of which could be prime targets. Most are located along the East Coast from New England all the way down to Florida, the Great Lakes/Rust Belt region, Appalachia, and the Deep South, with several more scattered along the Californian coast, Arizona, Texas, and the Seattle area.

Additionally, the United States possesses several ICBM (intercontinental ballistic missiles) missile bases that would serve as counterattack measures in the event of a nuclear war. Enemy forces would seek to eliminate these bases in addition to the nuclear power reactors described above.

Complicating things is that many of these ICBM bases are located in more remote regions of the country that are typically thought of as being safer (and more boring), including Montana, North Dakota, and Wyoming. That's in addition to other missile launch facilities scattered throughout the country as well, including along the Missouri River, the Appalachian Mountain range, and New England.

In short, fleeing to remote regions of the country, (such as the Appalachian mountains, the swamps of the Deep South, the Great Plains in the center of the country, or the Rocky Mountains in the Idaho-Montana-Wyoming-Utah region) will not automatically make you safe and outside of the danger zone.

The point of all of this is simple: there will be literally no 'safe zones' that will guarantee your survival after nuclear missiles have rained down over the country. Move into Montana or the Dakotas and you could find yourself in the middle of a nuclear blast targeting the ICBM bases. Move into Appalachia and you'll have to contend with being near the major cities, nuclear power plants, and retired hikers. You get the idea.

So rather than having the mindset that some areas in the country will be safe and other areas in the country will not be safe, have the mindset that nowhere in the country will be safe but that some areas will be 'not as dangerous' as others. These 'not as dangerous' areas will be literally anywhere that is at least one hundred miles away from a nuclear hotspot.

So where would the safest places (or more appropriately, the 'not as dangerous' areas) be with the above criteria in the United States?

In general, here are the likely 'not as dangerous areas' in the United States and the reasons for each one:

- Northern California/Eastern Oregon
  - o This is the only area near the West Coast of the United States that is not as likely to be directly targeted in a missile strike. Big cities and nuclear reactors/missile sites to the north in Washington state and south along the California coastline will be prime targets, so you may find yourself squeezed in between two hotspots (but then again, that likely can't be avoided anywhere in the country). Oregon currently has no nuclear power plants, and most of the state's military bases are located in the western part of the state rather than the East. Northern California does have a couple of

nuclear power plants, so make sure that you're safely away from each.

- Northern and Eastern Idaho/Southern Montana/Western Wyoming
  - Idaho, Montana, and Wyoming are commonly referred to as the 'American Redoubt' in SHTF circles because they are (mostly) away from any major hotspots, are fairly remote, have low population, and an abundance of natural resources, and are already favorite locations of those in the 'prepper' community due to the abundance of off-grid land for homesteads. You'll just want to be strategic about where exactly in these states you aim to be when a nuclear explosion goes off. For example, there are several ICBM sites in Montana that could be targeted. The capital city of Idaho, Boise, is growing rapidly and could be another potential nuclear hotspot.

- Great Plains States (South Dakota, Kansas, Nebraska, Oklahoma, Northern Texas)
  - The Great Plains States south of ICBM sites in North Dakota and clear of any military bases or major cities (such as Oklahoma City, Tulsa, Wichita, and Omaha) will likely be less likely to be hit in a nuclear attack. These areas are also more sparsely populated.

- Northern Arizona/Northern New Mexico

o   Northern Arizona and New Mexico are both less hot and arid than the southern regions of the states, which will make them more hospitable for surviving a long-term disaster scenario. They also contain fewer military bases, nuclear power plants, and other hot spots than down in the south.

- Central Mississippi and Alabama

    o   Central Mississippi and Alabama are probably among the least likely places to be directly impacted by nuclear warfare in the Deep South. Both of Alabama's two nuclear power plants are in the extreme north and south of the state, and Mississippi lone nuclear power plant is located in the southern part of the state. The central regions of both states are also farther away from the largest cities in both states and in the surrounding southern states as well.

- Northern Maine, New Hampshire, and Vermont (stay away from the coastline)

    o   In the Northeastern corner of the United States, northern Maine, New Hampshire, and Vermont are less likely to be targeted directly. This region is known for its sparsely populated forests and land that would be suitable for homesteads and off grid living. Just avoid the southern areas of these states as you'll be getting dangerously close to major population centers such as Boston as well as nuclear power plants and ICBM sites.

Again, living in the above areas does not guarantee that you will survive an upcoming nuclear conflict. But your odds of survival in the initial stages of the war will be increased. Only time will tell if you can survive the incoming nuclear war, the massive supply shortages, the advancing wildfires caused by the explosions, and the spreading of the radiation throughout the atmosphere.

If you live outside of the United States, apply the exact same 'formula' as we've gone over above. Identify every hotspot (or every major city or population center, military base) and try to live as far away from possible as each one. If you live in a very small country where it's not possible to be one hundred miles away from the nearest nuclear hotspot, just try to still live as far away as you reasonably can. Of course, we understand that not everyone will want to move their families to an area of absolutely no interest to avoid a conflict, and that if you do your friends may well take steps to get you institutionalized if you tell them this. But no one wants to die in a nuclear fireball either, so it's very much six of one and half a dozen of another.

On the opposite end of the spectrum, which cities in the United States would be the most likely targeted in the event of a nuclear war? We can't possibly predict the future, so we can't say with any definitive accuracy that one city will be attacked by a nuclear bomb while another will be spared.

But what we can do is assess which cities would be the most likely to be hit if hostile forces wanted to inflict the maximum amount of damage on the United States. Many public health and disaster preparedness experts agree that the six most likely targets of nuclear missiles in the United States are Washington D.C, Chicago, New York City, Houston, San Francisco, and Los Angeles. Essentially, wave goodbye to modern American cinema.

The reason is not only because of the massive populations in each of these cities, but also because each city is a major financial center and has numerous energy plants. The ramifications of just one of those cities being hit by a nuclear weapon would be felt all throughout the country for many years, most likely resulting in a near if not total economic collapse, massive supply shortages, and greatly increased global tensions if not all out war.

Alpha Strikes

There's also the possibility of enemy forces would attempt to launch an 'alpha strike' on the United States. An alpha strike is where one country or faction deploys tactical nuclear weapons against the nuclear bases of an enemy country. The goal is to eliminate the other country's nuclear weapons, thus rendering it near defenseless against further nuclear strikes and allowing the attacking country to deploy strategic nuclear weapons against major cities without fear of significant retaliation.

The only risk with an alpha strike strategy is that to be successful, the attacking country must destroy *all* of the defensive country's nuclear weapons in one fell swoop, or else nuclear retaliation and the threat of mutually assured destruction.

The logistics of launching an alpha strike is precisely why nuclear war never broke out between the US and USSR in the 20th century. Both countries had a strategy of launching an alpha first strike against the other, but because neither country was fully aware of every one of the sites of the other country's nuclear arsenal, neither could guarantee that they would annihilate the nuclear defenses of the other.

As a result, the only alternative was for neither country to deploy nuclear weapons against the other or for both sides to essentially destroy the other via mutually assured destruction, and if that doesn't make you feel safe in this world, then nothing will.

In today's world, there's also the risk that if one country armed with nuclear weapons successfully uses the alpha first strike against an opposing country, it will still face retaliation from allies of the latter nation.

Some countries that possess nuclear weapons do not contain enough nuclear weapons to launch a comprehensive nuclear strike against another nation. They only have the ability to launch retaliatory strikes after a nuclear war has been initiated. A prime example as of the time of this writing is China. While a major nuclear power, China simply does not possess enough (known) nuclear missiles to launch a complete alpha strike of a country armed with far more nuclear missiles, such as Russia or the United States. This means that China would almost certainly be in a defensive position if a nuclear war were to ever break out.

Other nuclear powers such as the UK, France, Israel, India, and Pakistan are in similar positions.

* * *

In short, you'll absolutely want to make sure that your home or nuclear survival shelter is away from any kind of a nuclear hot spot if you are serious about surviving a nuclear blast when it goes off.

Remember the following:

- Avoid being near any major cities or urban centers that are population centers and financial hubs.
- Avoid being near any major military bases or ICBM (intercontinental ballistic missile) sites that would be targeted.
- Avoid being near any major nuclear power plants.

If you currently live anywhere that is near any of the above hotspots, you'll want to seriously consider relocating to somewhere less near somewhere that's a potential target in a nuclear war. Remember not to give this as the primary reason for your relocation when applying for a mortgage, or the lender will either turn you down or ask to move in with you.

There are additional factors you'll want to take strongly into consideration as well in regard to where you decide to relocate and build your nuclear survival shelter (which we'll dive into in the next chapter).

Make sure that where you go meets the following criteria:

- Away from a major population centers and other major nuclear hotspots
- Offers an abundance of natural resources.
- Has suitable agricultural land and a suitable climate for growing crops?

Living somewhere that meets the above criteria (and being there at the time of the explosion) is the best precaution you can take against a nuclear strike and also the best way to ensure your survival immediately following a blast.

But again, simply being away from a nuclear strike will not guarantee your survival over the long term, and there are many more preparation and defensive measures that you will need to adopt. The best way to start is to construct a bunker or survival shelter that you and your family can retreat to following a disaster and ensuring that you have a healthy stockpile of food, water, and other necessities so you are prepared to deal with the upcoming supply shortages.

In the next chapter, we'll dive into how you can begin constructing your nuclear survival shelter to help you and your family survive a blast. Then, we'll start discussing how you can stockpile the shelter with enough supplies to ensure that you can outlast a major nuclear disaster.

CHAPTER FIVE:

BUILDING A NUCLEAR SHELTER

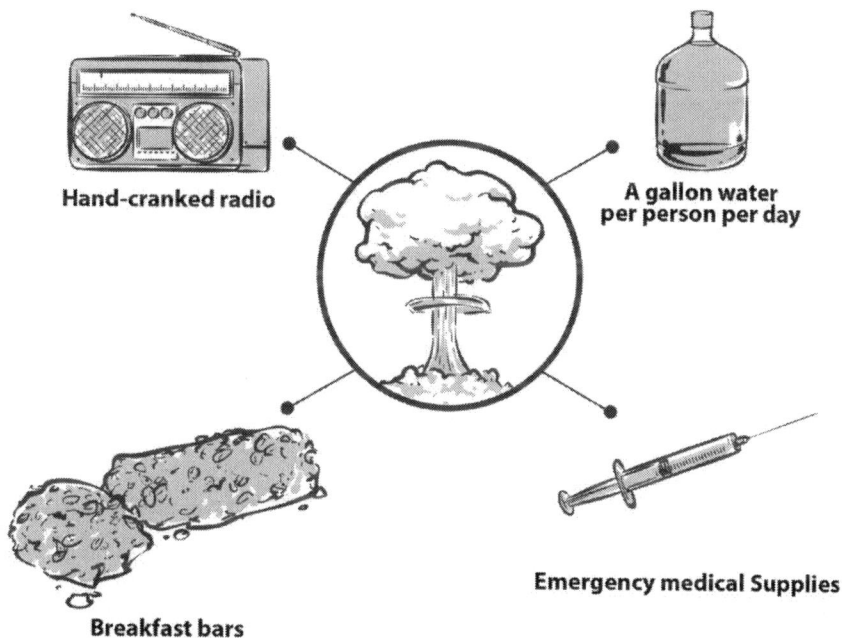

Hand-cranked radio

A gallon water per person per day

Breakfast bars

Emergency medical Supplies

After reading the preceding four chapters on the incredible damage that will be brought by a nuclear blast, the idea of constructing an underground bunker or structure for shelter should have come to mind. We've all read books or seen films or shows depicting 'preppers' getting ready for an end-of-the-world scenario like a nuclear blast by constructing a bunker or shelter for protection and then hoarding their items. It's important to recognize that when you begin constructing your shelter, many people will laugh at you or call you crazy. You will have the last laugh soon after they've turned into a pool of goo.

In reality, it isn't a bad idea, because having a properly constructed nuclear shelter can mean the difference between life-and-death following a nuclear explosion.

In this chapter, we will outline all the essential steps you need to take when making your own protective haven, from picking a suitable location and installing needed systems, right through stocking up on supplies. You can follow this process to ensure that your nuclear shelter is effective at keeping both yourself and those closest to you safe during any crisis. At this time, it's worth pointing out that this paragraph is rather technical and if you're not serious about nuclear war survival, you may want to breeze through it to avoid complicating your silly little brain.

Choose Your Location

Before beginning the construction process of your nuclear fallout shelter, it is important to pick out an appropriate location. Aim for a private and secure spot that has access to food and water sources, such as a plot of land out in the woods.

When selecting your subterranean refuge's position, consider its distance away from urbanized areas (try to ensure it is at least a hundred miles away from the nearest big city which could be a likely nuclear target), how easy it will be to get to during emergencies, plus any risk factors linked with possible radiation contamination exposure due to rising levels caused by potential blasts elsewhere on the land. Your selected location needs not only to provide safety precautions against the dangers around it but must also have enough land and space to suitably fit the individuals necessary when disaster strikes (both inside and outside of the bunker itself).

When selecting the proper place for a nuclear shelter, security and availability of resources are crucial. Stay away from sites that may be at risk of flooding or other natural disasters, as well as those close to combustible elements like trees or utility lines. Avoid building your shelter directly next to a lake, river, or any other body of water. Ensuring that it's within walking distance of a body of water should be fine, but just think twice about placing it directly next to a water source so you can guard against the risk of flooding. Keep in mind that flooding is possible even without a nuclear strike as well. These are all good tips for building in general and crucial advice for any property portfolio building, remember to look after your investments, even in the face of a global apocalypse.

Ensure the site you pick has convenient access with a strong base. Think about terrain features (ideally the surrounding forest or mounds of land will 'hide' your shelter area from any nearby roads) and how far it is situated from urban locations. Make sure your shelter is firmly built to provide complete protection against potential dangers.

Designing a Blueprint for Your Underground Bunker

To construct a secure and practical nuclear fallout shelter, you will need to put together an accurate blueprint. To maximize the space of your underground bunker, consider allocating 5–10 square feet per person. This is recommended by FEMA (Federal Emergency Management Agency) for hurricane or tornado shelters. Concentrate on efficiency when arranging its layout. Think about beds, cots, and mats alongside creating a bathroom section that can be divided off using clothes or blankets too. Do not overlook food storage either as you plan out your runaway shelter's structure. To maximize space, use bunk beds so you have extra space to stockpile food, water, medications, personal hygiene items, and other daily essentials.

The whole concept of making sure these fallout shelters or bunkers are sound revolves around drawing detailed blueprints with precise specifications while taking into account factors such as maximizing the amount of space available. Optimize spaces inside by putting together sensible plans including essential elements like food reserves. Consider other accommodations necessary for temporary survival within one's local area during times of crisis caused by any kind of nuclear disaster. This will ensure optimum protection against hazardous surroundings when facing unavoidable threats from unforeseen circumstances that fall beyond our control.

And remember, your nuclear shelter won't just prove useful as a precaution against a nuclear war. You can use it in virtually any other kind of disaster as well, whether it's a separate EMP attack, an economic collapse, political unrest, natural disaster, or the commissioning of yet another series of the *Big Bang Theory*.

Selecting the Best Building Material

When constructing an underground bunker, selecting the appropriate building materials is essential to ensure its structural integrity and ability to resist a nuclear blast (even if it's already hundreds of miles away from the nearest city that would be a likely target in a nuclear war). Steel-reinforced concrete is highly recommended due to its life span, compression power, and heat resistance. It offers superb longevity alongside robustness against extreme conditions such as that of any potential detonation events. LEGO is, unfortunately, not as suitable as you might at first think, but it is more fun, and you can even make your bunker Star Wars themed.

Alternatively, metal sheeting for your shelter could offer durability as well as water resistance. It's not as strong as steel-reinforced concrete, but it will be much more affordable and therefore more viable, and it will certainly be better than being exposed out into the open.

For a more cost-effective option, go with compacted soil or packed dirt for surrounding the bunker.

Remember that building a nuclear shelter can also be done with basic materials, and you don't have to invest a fortune into constructing a military-looking bunker if you don't have the financial resources. For instance, a simple trench covered in roofing logs and dirt (again, use compacted or packed dirt as the minimum) will form an effective pole-covered trench shelter that is both waterproof and radiation-proof, if put together correctly. To construct it, the roofing logs should have a crisscross pattern and the soil should be tightly packed around them for added protection. Walls of sufficient height (aim for at least six feet) must also be built.

Constructing any type of nuclear shelter requires sound knowledge of how to assemble these pieces appropriately to achieve optimum efficiency from its use during any potential crisis.

Excavation and Construction Techniques

Before you begin, be sure to prepare the area for your shelter by eliminating all vegetation and clearing an extra ten feet around the site where the bunker or structure will be built. Utilizing excavation machinery such as trenchers and excavators is a more effective option than manual labor or makeshift methods, so consider contracting this part out if you have the funds to do so. Construction machinery will also enable linear digging movement, which can also help when cutting roots or laying utility lines.

Safety precautions are key during this process. Sloping/benching, shoring up structures, and erecting trench shields will guarantee protection from cave-ins throughout the construction of the fallout shelter itself through the "cut and cover" method: (1) dig out a trench deep enough, (2) make structural supports where needed in it, (3) put down the bombproof fortification within the structure, then (4) fill everything back up with earth finally. Maintain safety at every point while remaining efficient.

When building a nuclear fallout shelter, you must be mindful of the depth. For safety reasons, this should not exceed 10 feet at the most. If any part of an exit is blocked off during such a disaster, then being able to manually excavate to clear a way out would become vital. Hence, forward planning and making sure that there's no excessive amount of depth involved in construction becomes paramount.

Installing Essential Systems

When setting up an underground bunker, air filtration is a critical part of ensuring the safety and comfort of anyone living inside. Air filtration will ensure that you can breathe properly, and that a single fart won't end up suffocating the entirety of your party. The size of the bunker should be considered when selecting equipment for this purpose. Ventilation and moisture control systems are also key components to ensure that living conditions remain pleasant within the space while waste removal services will make it possible to keep everything clean at all times. By carefully selecting each component according to your specific needs, you can create a well-functioning environment in your shelter.

- **Air Filtration System**

A reliable solution for air filtration in your bunker is an NBC (Nuclear, Biological and Chemical) system with a pump. This filters exterior air and releases pressure into the confined space to maintain positive relative pressure and prevents outside contaminants from entering. A hand-cranked or battery-operated setup promises clean recycled quality air every time. Additionally, make sure that you have instruments that can measure oxygen and carbon dioxide levels, which are critical factors needed for creating a safe atmosphere within your shelter during nuclear emergencies. This will immediately communicate to you if it's safe to remain in the shelter.

- **Ventilation and Moisture Control**

Ventilation and moisture control are imperative to preserving a wholesome environment in your bunker. Some strategies for achieving this include adding air vents for ventilation, installing insulation in the walls and ceilings so temperatures remain consistent, and setting up an NBC filtration system that will provide ample airflow as well as filter out dangerous substances. To keep everything dry within the bunker, try using dehumidifiers or putting in vapor barriers. It is critical to maintain temperature/moisture balance if you want occupants of the space to feel comfortable and safe.

- **Waste Removal and Composting Toilet**

As the great Queen Victoria once said, "everybody poops, now fetch me dinner."

To ensure hygienic waste disposal in a nuclear shelter, install an appropriate waste removal system. Go with a composting toilet because it will help reduce any unpleasant odors within the confined space of your bunker.

Throughout human history, literally millions of people have died due to poor sanitation practice so a proper system of safely dealing with human waste is more crucial than one might think.

To maintain cleanliness and ensure there are no health risks from poor sanitation practices during times of crisis or emergency, it's highly advisable to consider your waste removal system with care. Have a clear plan in place for how you will remove waste from your bunker. Always ensure that waste is buried at least two hundred feet away from the site of your bunker and any nearby water sources as well. Make sure that the waste is buried with at least one foot of dirt or soil covering it to keep flies and mosquitoes at bay (both of which can easily spread infections if they get into your waste and then fly back to come into contact with you or your family). It's probably worth marking where you've buried the waste as well, so you don't forget and, dig it back up and end up in poomageddon as well as the very real Armageddon the world is currently in.

- **Stocking up on Supplies and Provisions**

The chief purpose of your bunker is to provide yourself and your family protection from nuclear radiation and fallout. But the secondary purpose is to store a stockpile of supplies and ensure those supplies are kept protected against radiation as well. Filling your underground bunker with emergency supplies like bottled water, non-perishable foods, and medical items is essential for survival.

At the absolute minimum, you need to have at least one month's supply of food and water in your bunker. Food should be as long-lasting as it can be, prioritizing canned and preserved foods where possible. Powdered or dried food is also useful and can provide sustenance in a pinch. Remember not to buy SPAM however, because that's just nasty. Each person in your family will need at least one gallon of water per day, with a half-gallon to be used for drinking purposes to ensure proper hydration and another half-gallon to be used for cleaning and personal hygiene.

That's a lot of water to store (a hundred and twenty gallons), which is why (again) it's so crucial to maximize space in your bunker. A good strategy can be to have two primary rooms in your nuclear shelter: one room for living and sleeping, and another room exclusively for storage, most of which will be food and water.

- **Reinforcing and Concealing Your Nuclear Shelter**

You can further reinforce your nuclear survival shelter in the following ways:

Firstly, utilize sandbags or other improvised materials to fortify its foundation. Make sure that the walls and roof are securely bolstered to ensure it remains stable. Waterproofing the structure with rubberized asphalt will be good as well for superior coverage from external elements such as rainfall. Again, you need to ensure the stability and integrity of your structure over the long term and from outside elements.

Secondly, you should establish proper air circulation inside by strategically placing fans. Ensure that there is at least one fan per room in the shelter, with the fan ideally being in the corner so it can circulate air throughout the room.

Lastly, because this is very easy to overlook, do not forget about concealment. Constructing your bunker off-site, more than ten feet below ground level, will help preserve secrecy. The last thing you want is a load of mutated Jehovah's Witnesses knocking on your bunker all day long. You need to be strategic about where you choose to build the shelter. Selecting a property in the woods concealed by valleys, trees, and mounds of earth and requiring a long path of back dirt roads to reach will reduce the number of people who happen to stumble onto your property. Your shelter must be on a plot of land that cannot be easily seen or detected from any roads or highways at the absolute minimum.

Staying out of sight of potential adversaries (who will likely be looking above the surface) may be vital during a possible nuclear war or explosion circumstances because raiding and looting parties will be on the hunt scavenging for resources. Your bunker and its contents will become a prime target in the event it is detected. Reinforcing and concealing your bunker maximizes the safety and security of those individuals stationed within, making them valuable assets long-term.

- **Emergency Exit Strategies**

Having multiple emergency exit routes in a bunker is essential as a last-resort option. Make sure to install doors that open inward so they can be accessed if something falls and obstructs them. It's also advisable to create an additional underground escape route that can take you outside at least fifty or a hundred feet away from the bunker. This will hopefully allow you to sneak away if the bunker is discovered and comes under assault from raiding parties.

****

As you can hopefully tell, with the proper planning and materials, it is possible to construct a safe refuge for you and your family in the event of a nuclear explosion. The following components must be taken into account: selecting a hidden spot, equipping the shelter with the necessary utilities, bolstering its structural integrity with the measures we covered above, and loading up on necessities while ensuring that there is enough space for everything.

In the next chapter, we'll dive into a discussion of the most important items to stockpile in your nuclear shelter.

CHAPTER SIX:

ITEMS TO STOCK UP ON TO PREPARE FOR NUCLEAR WAR

1 **AVOID**

Avoid looking at the flash of light and keep mouth open during blast

2 **MOVE or SHELTER**

Move away or shelter underground or above the 9 floor of a building within 10-20 minutes

3 **MOVE CROSSWIND**

Move crosswind away from damaged buildings

4 **STAY COVERED**

Try to keep skin, mouth and nose covered

5 **DECONTAMINATE**

Remove clothing, rinse off with a hose and seek medical care ASAP

6 **12-24 HOURS**

Stay in your shelter for 12-24 hours or for as long as instructed by officials, then move in the direction officials advise

In the last chapter, we briefly touched upon stockpiling enough food, water, and other necessary supplies. We're going to discuss exactly what you need to stockpile in this chapter. This is the fun bit - shopping spree montage time!

It is of the utmost importance to always stay prepared by having a well-equipped survival kit in the event of a nuclear attack. In this chapter, we'll help guide you through putting together an effective and beneficial nuclear wartime emergency stockpile so that you can be adequately prepared for an incoming nuclear war. This includes food storage, water purification materials, and everything necessary for successful preparation against potential disasters.

You're now well aware of the devastating consequences of a nuclear explosion. You know that you are unlikely to safely resupply following a nuclear strike. Instead, you will have to rely on (A.) The items you have stockpiled. (B.) The items you can make or grow or replenish yourself. (C.) The items you can scavenge (while competing against other people in the process). Focusing on A so you can keep B and C to a minimum should be your goal.

Having suitable storage arrangements beforehand can help to ensure your survival. Staying indoors away from exterior walls is absolutely vital as it significantly decreases your chance of absorbing too much hazardous radiation should it be present outside your dwelling area.

Assembling a survival kit and stockpile of supplies (like we discussed in the last chapter) within your shelter should also prove useful. You'll need to have enough food and water supplies along with other materials required per person (plus pets) for at least one month following the attack. Plan on setting aside a month's worth of provisions at first and then aim to grow your stockpile from there.

When constructing a nuclear war survival kit, it is essential to include instruments and supplies that can help you remain sound and protected during the aftermath. Think of all angles and possibilities that may occur when you are cut off from the sources of assistance you typically rely on. Customize your provisions according to each family member's requirements, including medications, and prescriptions, dietary restrictions, allergies, or other needs they may have. Do your planning and preparation now, and you'll be grateful for it later.

****

Having the proper amount of food and water in your survival stockpile is necessary to survive following a nuclear attack. This is because the supply chains will shut down and you'll no longer be able to resupply yourself from grocery stores.

So, what kinds of food should you focus on stockpile? Include foods with high calories that are filled with carbohydrates, proteins, and adequate H2O for each individual for three days. Canned meals, dried fruits, or granola bars are ideal choices as non-perishable items as these have an extensive shelf life and also come packed with nutrition. Low-effort meals (for example instant ravioli or soup) are excellent canned food options as well that require minimal preparation yet provide vital calories and nutrients you will need to consume while staying inside due to radiation exposure dangers. Essentially, you're going to be eating like an English person in the 1960s... or the 1970s... or the 2010s really, their food isn't the best.

Provided they weren't directly exposed to radiation in any way during the initial blast, these pre-packaged supplies will remain consumable without issue following a nuclear strike. Any item safeguarded inside an unharmed building is still safe to use or consume. This is a key concept to remember, and it underscores why it's so important to stockpile as much food and water as you can. Remember: *you can never stockpile enough*. After building your initial stockpile, continuously add onto it as you go about your life.

Put together a month's supply of food, and then make it a habit to add one or two cans of food to it weekly going onward. You'll be surprised at how fast your stockpile grows using this strategy, and it's a concept you can apply to stockpiling other necessities as well (such as personal hygiene items, ammunition, medications, and so on).

In the event of a nuclear disaster, consume perishable supplies first and leave the non-perishables for later. This will help ensure that there will be enough sustenance for yourself and your family during the long period spent inside. Don't forget about pet food if any animal companions will be joining you too.

When it comes time to store these essential commodities, safety measures should be taken to ensure the integrity of the goods over the long term. You won't be able to replenish your food supply so easily, so making sure that the proper precautions are taken to protect your food from environmental contamination such as moisture must be a top priority for you.

To that end, stock items in cool dry places such as basements or pantries on lower floors, keep containers airtight to prevent contamination from bacteria spreading, and regularly go through all provisions, using older ones and then adding newer products. Tupperware may very well be the unsung hero of surviving the apocalypse. Every six months, do a complete stock take of all items in your kit and check for anything that may need replacing due to expiry or malfunction. Nuclear war or no, you don't want to end up vomiting because of some gone off beans.

As mentioned, in the event of a nuclear disaster, it is essential to have access to a secure and reliable water supply. Ensure each person in your household has enough clean drinking water stored for at least three days' worth if possible. Keep containers (contaminant-free) somewhere cool and dim like in an underground pantry/basement so any ready supplies remain fresh during times of emergency.

Home filtration systems come into play to continue vital functions even when municipal support has been cut off due to chaos following the disaster. There are several ways this can be achieved: using reverse osmosis filters that remove impurities by employing semi-permeable membranes, through ion exchange processes that utilize specialized resins for eliminating pollutants, distillation boiling of contaminated liquid then returning in its purified form when steam condenses back into H2O, or with chemical tablets included in purifying solutions. Use plastic containers that have been disinfected with bleach to store purified distilled drinking water safely.

****

Other key items to stockpile include battery-operated radios and flashlights. Also consider hard-copy maps for navigation, with matches attached, so if you need to journey away from the area, you can do so swiftly. While you need to be prepared to stay for long periods in your bunker, also prepare for situations where you may need to evacuate by foot to escape danger, including specific points of evacuation designated by authorities. A blanket or sleeping bag might be useful along with weather-proof clothing. Consider tools like shovels or pickaxes and fire starter materials.

Solar-powered radios are a great tool for reaching wider broadcasting networks beyond your immediate area. Don't forget to have solar-powered chargers on hand to power up devices such as flashlights or cell phones, which will be necessary due to the long-term power outages and collapse of the power grid that will result after a nuclear strike.

Stockpile first aid basics and radiation care materials such as potassium iodide and dosimeters. These are especially important medications to stockpile in preparation for nuclear fallout. Potassium iodide is a salt that helps protect the thyroid gland from radioactive iodine released by bombs and can lower the risk of cancer that can set in from prolonged radiation exposure later. It's worth noting that this shouldn't be used as liberally as a table salt substitute. Meanwhile, a dosimeter measures external radiation in our body, so we know when protective steps need to be taken. Kits containing KIO3 (potassium iodate) tablets and RADTriage50 personal dosimeters are available readymade just about anywhere that sells survival equipment and items online these days.

Personal grooming is going to remain important, as health complications can arise from not maintaining good hygiene and grooming. However, consider the upcoming apocalypse a chance to branch out into new hairstyles and motifs such as:

- Leader of a biker gang.
- Supervisor at a hipster coffee shop.
- Dreadlocked hippie.
- Bald and beautiful.

Have fun with it!

Checklist of Survival Items to Include in Your Survival Shelter

With all of the above information in mind, here's a complete checklist of survival items that you should try to stockpile (ideally in your nuclear survival shelter). Remember that your stockpile needs to cover all of your bases, and to that end, it should include plenty of food and water to ensure that you can stay fueled and hydrated.

Food and Water:

When storing food and water, make sure that you accomplish three things:

1. Store enough food and water to last you and your family for a designated period of time.
2. Store enough variety that your nutritional needs are met.
3. Ensure that you store foods that are long-lasting and non-perishable for extended periods of time when stored at normal room temperature.

- 120 Gallons of Water

  o This figure is based on storing 1 gallon of water per person for a typical family of four for a month. The easiest way to store this much water will be in two fifty-five-gallon drums plus additional water bottles.

  o Also note that the 120 gallons will go by quick between drinking, using with meals (such as flour and pasta), and cleaning/personal hygiene use. Water truly is something that you can never store enough of.

○ Additionally, make sure that you store a family-sized water filter, personal filter devices (one per family member) and several containers of water purification tablets with iodide.

- All-Purpose Flour

○ Mix all-purpose flour with water and there is no shortage of meals you can bake. Additional baking items to consider storing are baking soda, corn starch, yeast, and vanilla extract.

- Canned Foods

○ Canned foods can last indefinitely when unopened and stored at normal room temperature. Store canned fruits, canned beans and vegetables, and canned meats.

- Coffee/Tea

○ It may not be essential, but coffee and tea will help keep your morale up if you drink either one. You merely need to combine it with water.

- Instant Mashed Potatoes

○ Instant mashed potatoes can maintain normal quality while being stored at normal room temperature for up to two years.

- Olive Oil/Vegetable Oil
  - You'll find olive or vegetable oil will come in handy when cooking meals, depending on how you've used it, oil can also be reusable.
- Pasta
  - Pasta is long lasting and can be prepared simply by adding it to water.
- Peanut Butter
  - Peanut butter is an excellent source of protein but avoid it if you or anyone else in your family has serious allergies.
- Rice
  - Make sure you go with white rice, which is much more long-lasting than brown rice.
- Salt and Pepper / Spices
  - While not necessary, adding salt and pepper to your meals will help enhance the flavor, which can boost morale. Bland food is never worth looking forward to and spices can really enhance your eating experience.

Feel free to include more non-perishable foods depending on what you and your family's preferences are. You can also consider investing in pre-made food kits. These kits are commonly designed for either individuals or families and have enough food to last for between a month to over a year depending on the kit that you get. While expensive and commonly running to hundreds of dollars, they provide a complete and efficient way for food storage and can complement your personal storage of the above items. It'll be worth investing in recipe books to help spark some creativity, or even work on doomsday recipes yourself. Just because there's an apocalypse out there, that doesn't mean your family has to suffer poor cuisine here. Who knows, a nuclear Michelin star inspector might come knocking before too long.

Additionally, don't forget to include a complete cooking set in your survival shelter separate from the existing set that you have in your kitchen at home. You'll want to store pots and pans of varying sizes, a good Dutch oven, a good cast iron skillet, bowls, plates, cooking utensils, kitchen knives, and cooking spatulas and spoons.

Comfort and Sleeping Items

The following items are important for staying warm and ensuring that you can get a good night's sleep. Becoming fully rested each night is vitally important for making sure that you can function properly and think clearly.

- Blankets
- Clothing
  - Make sure that each family member has at least three sets of clothing set aside in your survival shelter. This

means three sets of jackets/sweatshirt, shirts, pants, shorts, underwear, and socks.

- Pillows
- Sleeping Bags
- Sleeping Cots or Mattresses (one per family member)

First Aid Kit

First Aid Kits are going to be crucial as regular access to doctors and hospitals will likely be removed. Make sure you have a decent array of healthcare books to refer to, and a decent stockpile of medicine, both over the counter and prescription. Avoid buying a pre-made complete first aid kit and instead assemble your own custom first aid kit by buying the items individually. This way, you will become more intimately familiar with item in your first aid kit:

- Adhesive Tape
- Antibiotics
- Antibiotic Ointment
- Aspirin
- Bandages (of varying sizes)
- Blister Treatment Kit
- Duct Tape (can be used to help fasten and secure splints over fractured limbs)
- Elastic Wrap Bandages
- Eye Drops
- First Aid Manual
- Gauze Pads (varying sizes)

71

- Ibuprofen
- Ice Packs
- Medical Gloves
- Medical Tweezers
- Mylar Blanket
- Prescription Medications (if applicable)
- Splints (larger ones for limbs and smaller ones for fingers and toes)
- Suture Threads and Needles
- Sting Kit
- Tourniquet
  - Go for a combat tourniquet, as it will be more effective at preventing blood flow in open wounds.
- Tylenol

Personal Hygiene/Cleaning

In general, the importance of personal hygiene and general cleanliness is very overlooked when it comes to preparing for a survival situation in general. Staying clean is necessary for stopping the spread of diseases and preventing your partner from finding you physically repulsive to be around. Store each of the following at minimum:

- Baby Wipes
- Cotton Bals
- Deodorant
- Dishwashing Soap

- Garbage Bags
- Laundry Detergent
- Q-Tips
- Razor Blades
- Shampoo (dry and liquid)
- Shaving Cream
- Soap Bars
- Toilet Paper
- Vaseline
- Wet Wipes

Just like how can never truly store enough food and water in preparation for a disaster, you can truly never store enough of the above.

Protective Clothing

Protecting your physical person is of the utmost importance for shielding yourself from radiation in a nuclear fallout. Make sure that each person in your family or survival group has each of the following:

- Boots
  - Look for good hiking boots that offer excellent traction and fully cover your ankle and lower legs.
- Coveralls
  - Coveralls have a similar effect to a hazmat suit. They should cover your entire body except for your hands and your face.

- Gas Masks

  o Look for masks that are constructed out of bromobutyl rubber - the MIRA CM-6M gas mask is a good option.

- Goggles

  o Go for industrial safety goggles.

- Gloves

  o Go with nitrile exam gloves. Storing additional leather work gloves would be a good idea as well because they offer superior durability.

Nuclear War-specific Items:

The following items are essential to store specifically as preparation for the aftermath of a nuclear war, rather than a more generalized disaster. The items may be difficult to get hold of at times but take your time and then find the right products for you.

- Personal Dosimeters

  o RADTriage50 is a good choice.

- Potassium Iodide (K103)

  o K103

- Radio (Hand Crank model)
- Surgical Masks

Miscellaneous Survival Items:

The following items collectively don't all fall under one category, but will be necessary to store nonetheless:

- Batteries
  - Make a list of every battery-powered item you have (such as flashlights, radios, etc.) and make sure you have at least one pack of batteries set aside for each item.
- Bottle Openers
- Candles
- Can Openers
- Cards and Games (though don't choose Monopoly, the last thing you want is a full-scale argument in the middle of the apocalypse.)
- Compass
- Documents
  - Copies of any family/government/medical/property-related documents should be stored and stashed away in waterproof bags.
- Fire Starting Devices
  - Go with a variety of fire-starting devices, including magnesium flint strikers, matches, and personal lighters.
  - Make sure you store plenty of kindling as well to make it easy to get a fire going. Cotton balls or Q-Tips

coated in Vaseline are very flammable. Old newspapers, moss, and twigs are also good to collect in this regard.

- Flares
- Flashlights (at least one per family member)
- Fire Extinguisher (at least two)
- Hatchets/Tomahawks
- Knives

   o Store several knives, including cooking knives, fixed-blade knives, and folding knives that you can stash away in your pockets.

- Lantern (plus fuel for powering it)
- Map

   o Don't think that you can just rely on GPS devices (an EMP would knock them out)

- Plastic Bags
- Plastic Sheeting and Tarps
- Rope

   o Try to set aside at least two hundred and fifty feet worth of rope and paracord.

- Splitting Maul/Axe
- Whistle

Tools:

Ideally you should have a complete toolkit set aside in your nuclear survival shelter. Make sure this tool kit includes the following items at the bare minimum:

- Duct Tape
- Hammer
- Nails
- Pliers
- Screwdriver
- Screws
- Shovels
    - Go with one compact multi-purpose model and one larger shovel.
- Wire Saw
- Wrench

Remember that you should customize your survival storage to suit your needs. Use the above list as a reference point, but absolutely feel free to include more items as you see fit. For example, if you have an infant in the family, you'll want to include plenty of baby-related items as you can, and you'll also want to store more clothing in increasing sizes to prepare for the baby's growth in the future.

****

Assembling an adequate nuclear war survival kit is essential in safeguarding yourself and those close to you during a crisis. You should include the right tools, equipment, resources, water supply, and food items. Notably, equipment to help you stay informed about events happening outside can make all the difference. Don't wait until it's too late - protect your family by being prepared beforehand for the unfortunate circumstances arising from a potential nuclear attack.

To make sure everyone survives, keep your family informed about the news regarding potential threats surrounding nuclear conflict so they can plan accordingly. This includes having plans for evacuation measures if necessary as well as back-up methods to communicate with friends throughout any event linked to this type of warfare. Though it's important not to bang on about it too much, otherwise all children will become constantly frightened, and your partner may very well roll their eyes so much that they fall out of their heads.

Remember, in the event of a nuclear strike, local authorities may suggest that you remain indoors for up to four weeks. This entails staying in your home or another secure area with enough provisions such as food, water, and other supplies to last for an entire month. It is crucial to have all these items ready before any potential attack involving nuclear weapons occurs as you won't necessarily have much time to gather items.

Taking action in the above manner now may give you peace of mind later on. No one wants to think about what life would be like after a nuclear war, but we must be prepared regardless, nonetheless. The actions that you take today will be what saves you and your family tomorrow.

Remember: taking precautions is always better than being taken off guard while facing any sort of circumstance involving nuclear warfare. Be properly equipped with supplies necessary for surviving a potentially fatal scenario like this so you don't have to worry if the time comes. Remain vigilant and start preparing now. There's an old saying to pray for the best but to prepare for the worst. When the worst happens, you'll be glad you prepared.

Having said all of this, do not under any circumstances bring your guitar into the bunker. The last thing your family or friends need is being subjected to the sound of your attempting the solo from *Don't Stop* by Fleetwood Mac, 60 times in a row and failing to play the pinch harmonics. No-one needs it, no one wants it. Just don't.

CHAPTER SEVEN:

WHAT TO DO WHEN A NUCLEAR ATTACK IS IMMINENT

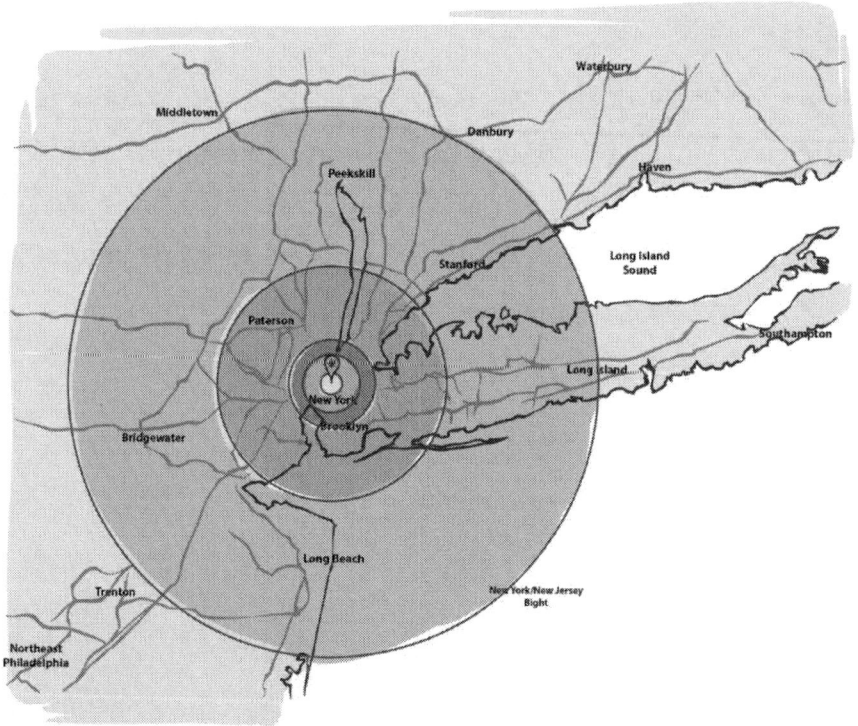

What will ultimately save your life in a nuclear attack is not just how you prepare for the attack in the months and years beforehand (even though that's important) but also what you do when you believe or are informed that an attack is imminent. Running around screaming is acceptable for a short amount of time, but ultimately isn't going to save anyone's life.

It is vital to be mindful of the telltale signs of a potential nuclear incident. Official warnings may be delivered by the local authorities, alterations in DEFCON levels can become visible and sent out to the general public as a pre-warning, and international tensions will almost certainly heighten leading up to the attack. This is why it's so important to remain aware of what's going on in regard to global affairs. Keep yourself informed with reliable news sites, avoiding conspiracy news outlets or inflammatory organizations. You don't want to be informed about Armageddon in the same paragraph as rumors about the casting of the new Spiderman. There will almost certainly be talk of a potential nuclear blast before it occurs. If two countries armed with nuclear weapons start becoming hostile to one another or go directly to war, there may be talk of either of them using nuclear weapons.

To stay informed during such situations, tune into news broadcasts or alerts sent out by emergency response personnel if talk of a nuclear strike amplifies. In the event of an all-out war with nukes, national disaster recovery plans will kick off, including action taken by authorities at the federal, state, and local levels.

When a nuclear attack is imminent, you must take swift and immediate action to ensure the safety of yourself and those nearby. Immediately abandon what you are doing and focus on the safety of yourself and your loved ones. Video games can wait, movies must be turned off, and your new novel can be completed another time. Find shelter, cover any exposed areas of skin, and gather essential items quickly. Hopefully, you already have a shelter and stockpile of items that you can turn to like we've covered in the preceding chapters as well.

Do this with immediate urgency so you can remain safe from the impending blast. It will also help if any necessary supplies such as food or water for long-term protection against radiation have been gathered beforehand in case there isn't sufficient time when an alert has been issued.

As soon as you receive a nuclear attack warning, you must find shelter indoors while trying to get as far away from the blast as possible. As a rule, you want to be a minimum of ten miles away from the blast site, but even then, you'll feel the effects and become exposed to radiation. Finding shelter in fifteen minutes or less is of the utmost importance. Concrete structures are ideal for shielding against radiation and fallout from an atomic blast. Aim for the lowest possible room like a cellar or basement. Being under a cover can be ten times safer than being exposed outside, even if it's just half underground in a wood-frame construction home. As we talked about earlier, even a minimalist shelter will be better than having no shelter at all, even if it lacks the extra reinforcement of steel or concrete.

A shelter gives protection from potential radiation caused by the detonation's fallout, which will come into contact with people who are outdoors. If you can't access the survival shelter or bunker that you have prepared, suitable refuge should be located inside buildings such as schools and offices that have minimal windows, if any at all. Particularly useful are buildings with basements where occupants can temporarily take cover.

When selecting an appropriate location for above-ground structures to seek safety, stay clear of doorways and narrow halls since they serve as wind tunnels that will amplify shockwaves, which could pose a risk. Choose large open spaces and utilize walls for shielding when feasible before the fallout arrives. Lastly, try not to enter areas containing glass panes until after the fallout has finished.

If you are caught outside with no cover, lie flat on the ground with your hands tucked under. This is to ensure safety against intense heat or flying debris.

In the event of a nuclear attack, it is critical to protect uncovered body parts from radiation and debris. Put on clothing that covers your head down to your toes for protection. Also, wear a mask or cloth over your face to protect against intense light during the blast. If you are outside when the blast happens, take off any contaminated items right away and rinse yourself completely to rid of radioactive residue particles. Yes, someone might see you naked and they may well remark about the mole on your butt, but you'll have to get over it. Taking these steps will help minimize the risks associated with exposure to radioactivity following a nuclear explosion.

Radiation exposure is highest for those in close proximity to the blast site. Symptoms and consequences include acute radiation syndrome (ARS), skin burns, eye damage, and malignancy - all of which could lead to painful and serious health problems associated with radiation sickness in the weeks, months, or years following the blast itself. Local emergency management may distribute potassium iodide (KI) pills to protect against radioactive iodine, but as mentioned in the previous chapter, be sure to stock up yourself just in case none are distributed due to the collapse of emergency first response services. People with certain medical conditions should avoid them as they may have an adverse reaction, so do your research to confirm you won't have any reactions.

The amount of danger posed by nuclear fallout consisting of small sandy particles decreases substantially within one hour after detonation, dropping from 100% down 55%. This is repeated at twenty-four hours when it drops by 80%. To ensure safety during this period following a nuclear attack or war involving these weapons, knowledge about symptoms and effects is essential so you can take steps toward reducing your own exposure risk as well as protecting friends/family members.

****

Stay informed and take direction from emergency response officials. Depending on the scale, government may still be functioning and will have ideas of how to save as many lives as possible. You don't want to isolate yourself if greater help is available from the authorities. If suggested, evacuation or relocation may be necessary. People must go to designated public shelters if they are advised to evacuate during this type of crisis. All risk factors must be considered before making any decisions concerning movement in times like this when tensions surrounding an impending nuclear war exist.

To cope with the mental health issues associated with a nuclear blast or war, survivors should reach out and establish coping methods such as talking about their emotions when needed. Receiving advice from visiting counselors can be beneficial too. By taking action, they will have better chances at starting recovery processes that may lead them back to having hope again, one step at a time.

For surviving in the long-term following a nuclear blast involving weapons, preparation and planning are vital. As we've already covered, ensuring adequate supplies of food and water, safeguarding your shelter properly and monitoring news sources for relevant information should be prioritized to increase chances of safety after an attack with atomic bombs or warheads. Having as much of this in place before the blast will allow you to focus on other survival factors - and there'll be a lot to do!

To remain up to date about the impending threat of a nuclear disaster, there are resources available, like the website belonging to the Centers for Disease Control at emergency.cdc.gov. You can also contact pertinent entities concerning radiation exposure plus disaster response programs. By seeking such knowledge, you can enhance your odds of surviving nuclear warfare.

****

In short, in order to be ready in the face of a nuclear attack, it is important to recognize signs ahead of time, act swiftly, and plan for long-term protection. Just as important as staying safe during an attack is staying informed on current affairs in advance to give you an edge when disaster strikes.

Keep the following tips in mind:

- Citizens of the United States can get a Wireless Emergency Alert concerning a nuclear attack. Authorities may issue warnings, the DEFCON level could change, and there might be escalating geopolitical tensions as warning signs of a possible nuclear attack. However, there's also the reality that there might not be any warning at all.
- To prepare, ensure all of your windows and doors are properly secured. Check the fireplace damper is closed as well. To protect against radiation plumes quickly if needed, seal off entryways such as vents or door/window frames with duct tape and plastic sheeting for a brief time period.
- Have potassium iodide on hand to safeguard your thyroid gland. Store this in an emergency supply kit that is kept in an easily retrievable location so that they are

available instantly if necessary. This will help you and your family stay safe during this kind of situation.

- Individuals situated two miles or away from a blast may be able to remain safe, provided that they are capable of finding appropriate shelter.

Next, we'll dive into how you should act in the ongoing aftermath of a nuclear attack after you survive the initial blast.

CHAPTER EIGHT:

HOW TO REACT IN THE AFTERMATH OF A NUCLEAR EXPLOSION

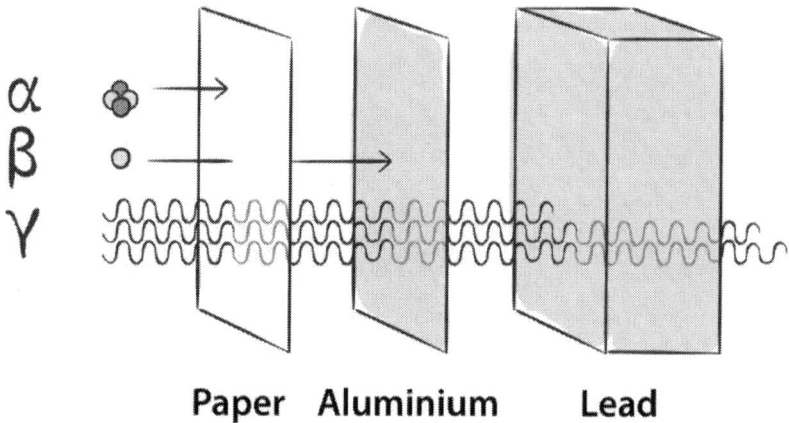

α

β

γ

Paper   Aluminium   Lead

Knowing the characteristics of radioactive fallout and the variety of radioactive elements that may be discharged during a nuclear occurrence is imperative for your survival post-nuclear blast. Radioactive contamination will permeate the surrounding environment in a multi-mile radius, presenting serious health hazards to anyone and everyone who is exposed to it. What doesn't kill you right away very well may kill you down the road, like living almost solely off Papa John's in your 20's.

In a nuclear attack, harmful radioactive particles are emitted during the resulting radioactive decay. Alpha particles, beta particles, and gamma rays produce radiation, which can cause detrimental effects on living cells and genetic material. In other words, it can infect your body and slowly eat away at you, resulting in a decrease in your muscle mass and cancerous tumors.

When exposed to a nuclear blast, you will always be at risk of suffering severe and damaging burns that increase in severity depending on your proximity to the site. Radiation released from a nuclear weapon puts those close by at an increased chance for ARS (acute radiation syndrome) or radiation sickness symptoms.

****

In case of a warning of radiation danger, rush inside the nearest building while staying away from any windows on your way in. If taking cover in a multi-story building, select a central location preferably not on the top or bottom floors and make use of natural light where possible, offering the optimum view of your surroundings.

If you fail to find adequate permanent shelter, safeguarding yourself from debris and heat is essential to avoid any risk of severe harm. To shield your vision against radiation hazards, be sure to avert your gaze and shut your eyes tightly.

Keep low on the ground to guard skin from being directly exposed and protect it from any airborne debris from crumbling structures. Use any structure available to block exposure.

When the pressure wave has died down, find refuge. Once the initial chaos has passed and even once you've found shelter, it's important to continue to manage your exposure to radioactive fallout. You might feel compelled to go outside and see what's happening but stay indoors for at least three days (more on this in a bit). Live your life like you've had a breakup, eat lots of food, watch the news, and do a lot of crying. Staying inside is your safest option.

To make sure radioactive particles do not enter your shelter, ensure all windows and doors are securely shut and sealed. Utilizing duct tape or plastic sheeting should help seal any small openings that exist. Turning off the ventilation system can prevent contaminated outside air from infiltrating inside your safe space to minimize potential exposure.

****

If possible, monitor radio and television broadcasts closely for updates and guidance. Keeping yourself updated with developments during a nuclear emergency is essential. A battery-operated or hand-crank-powered radio is one way to get reliable information. Be wary of non-government directives, you don't want to follow a bizarre conspiracy theory because you ended up tuning into Fox News by accident.

Listening and adhering strictly to guidelines given out by authorities will help you stay safe and secure as radiation fallout takes place. Directives may include instructions on when to evacuate, where to go, and what items you need for your journey. If an individual cannot manage to leave the area entirely, then following safety guidelines established by officials will help keep them safe during this crisis.

For an evacuation to go smoothly, it is essential that safe routes and places are planned beforehand. Get advice from local authorities, maps, and other sources regarding potential secure paths or spots. Think about regions not directly in the line of fallout, such as highland zones or areas protected by mountains or any kind of natural obstacles. When looking at likely routes to get to our survival shelter or bug-out location, take into consideration components like distance to destination, landscape, accessibility of resources, and chances of exposure to hazardous materials/radiation.

Additionally, try to have a minimum of three routes for getting to your designated location, as well as alternative routes for getting between routes in case you have to abandon any of them. Anything could happen in the immediate aftermath of the explosion and as Robert Baden-Powell once said, "Be Prepared." It's a short quote, but you get it.

****

How you act in the immediate aftermath of a nuclear incident is vital for your long-term survival. The radiation levels will always be the strongest in the hours and days following an attack but decrease significantly afterwards. Protecting yourself in the opening hours and days of the attack can pay dividends in ensuring your survival over the long term.

Keep the following tips in mind:

- Stay inside for at least twenty-four hours after a nuclear explosion. Radiation levels can decrease rapidly during this time, from as much as 1,000 roentgen/hour to as little as 10 roentgen/hour in the first three days. This doesn't mean that you will become immune to radiation within three days, but it does mean the danger level will lower significantly. Remember and apply the adage: "Three Days Indoors" following a nuclear strike and your chances of survival will rise tremendously. This isn't the COVID lockdown, there's no going outside for your daily walk here!

- Remaining in the most protective location (basement or center of a large building) will further help reduce exposure. Wait for instructions from the authorities before leaving the shelter.

- In the event of a radiation emergency, make sure that all windows and doors in your home leading outside are kept fully shut. Turn off any conditioners, fans, or any forced-air heating units as well. To ensure protection against possible contamination caused by passing plumes of radioactive material, use duct tape and plastic sheeting for sealing up openings. Make sure that there are absolutely no cracks in your windows or doors leading outside that can allow air to come in because if it does, radiation will come in with it.

- Ensure your pets and service animals remain indoors while the danger persists. Animals are subject to the same risks from exposure to unsafe levels of radioactivity as humans, and the loss of a pet in a nuclear blast can be an immense blow on top of the trauma and shock of what's happening.
- It is wise to avoid consuming any food directly exposed to the open air during the immediate aftermath.

In the next chapter, we'll dive into the deadly effects of nuclear radiation and how to keep yourself properly protected and sanitized.

CHAPTER NINE:

UNDERSTANDING NUCLEAR RADIATION AND HOW TO KEEP YOURSELF SANITIZED

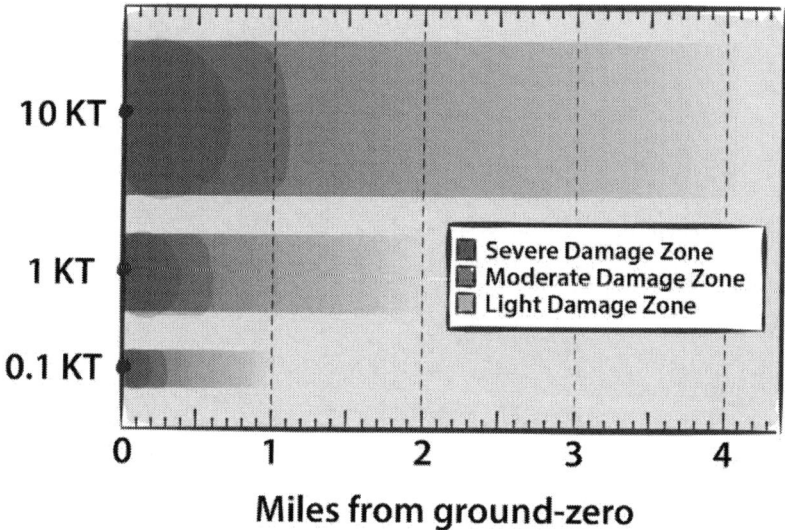

Miles from ground-zero

Radiation is a scary thing. We're constantly exposed to it, but it has the potential to kill you if you're unlucky. Nuclear radiation can be divided into two primary categories: ionizing radiation and non-ionizing radiation.

- Ionizing radiation involves particles that carry enough energy to form ions by removing electrons from atoms or molecules.
- Non-ionizing radiation does not cause atomic changes, but it can still have harmful physical or biological effects on your body.

The different forms of nuclear radiation all have different levels of penetration that require various protective measures to guard against.

1. Alpha particles are the least penetrating, with two protons and two neutrons composing them.
2. Beta particles (high-speed electrons or positrons) follow closely behind being more penetrating than alpha but also less so than gamma rays.
3. Gamma rays hold great potential for deep-reaching permeation, while neutrons released during nuclear accidents possess greater strength compared to alphas, and yet have lesser capability when compared to gammas.

So how can you protect yourself from these particles? Brick and concrete walls will diminish some effects from particularly strong gamma-ray exposure. However, neutrons can still find their way through. Despite this, concrete shielding should not be underestimated as a protective measure. It will properly shield you against *most* of the radiation that comes your way, which is why a concrete and steel nuclear shelter is the best bet for a structure that can properly guard you against nuclear fallout. Think of yourself as one of the little pigs, and the radiation as the big bad wolf. If you make your shelter from poor materials, then the big bad radiated wolf will easily find its way in and kill you mercilessly. Good luck reading that story to any children without thinking about nuclear weaponry now.

****

Radiation can cause a variety of maladies, injuries and sicknesses that depend on the level of exposure. The effects can be mild such as a weakened immune system and nausea or they can be severe resulting in death within days or weeks. To defend yourself and your loved ones from the effects of nuclear radiation, implement the basic principles for radiation protection:

Minimize how long you spend around a source of radiation to help lessen any risk associated with being exposed over an extended period. This sounds obvious, but it's about being proactive. Increasing the distance between yourself and known sources of nuclear radiation will also go to great lengths to keep you safe.

Many materials you may already have access to, such as lead or concrete, can provide effective shields that deflect or absorb incoming rays when applied correctly.

Defending yourself from radiation can be carried out in different ways such as relocation, erecting barriers such as walls or buildings to protect yourself against the blast, and wearing protective clothing over your entire body, especially your hands, head, and face.

The importance of shielding is pretty straightforward: it creates a barrier between the source of radiation and you. This is precisely why constructing a survival shelter is so important for you and your family and is not something to take lightly. It allows for a reduction or even an avoidance of exposure, with materials such as lead aprons or concrete walls absorbing ionizing radiation.

Even aluminum foil, which is available in most homes and grocery stores, can be very effective in preventing alpha radiation from reaching the person. Depending on its quality, aluminum foil can even shield gamma radiation if there are nineteen inches or more between the individual and the source. A thickness of up to 5 mm alone will block out beta radiation entirely. Turn yourself into an aluminum mummy, if possible, do whatever it takes to keep the radiation out!

If you're stockpiling aluminum foil, make sure you have a good reason for the cashier. Say that you're baking the world's largest brownie or something, make it a good excuse.

****

As the bomb was detonated and radiation is spreading through the air like the bad fart that it is, decontamination measures are going to be crucial. Decontamination procedures are essential to minimize exposure to radioactive particles and reduce associated health risks. Simply protecting yourself with aluminum foil and other barriers as we talked about above won't be enough to guarantee protection from radiation.

Decontamination steps include showering, discarding contaminated clothing, and proper handling and disposal of any waste that may be irradiated with radiation.

To ensure successful containment, follow these measures carefully for all those exposed or potentially exposed to fallout from the blast zone:

1. Take off your outer layer of clothing and seal it away using plastic bags so there won't be contamination.

2. Bathe yourself in clean water as soon as possible to remove any radioactive particles that have attached themselves. Warm water and soap should be employed for a thorough cleansing, paying special attention to the hands, face, and hair. Don't worry about having a shave, which can wait until later, plus beards are cool nowadays.

3. Use a mild soap without conditioner. After you have emerged out of the water and dried off, your face and hands should then be disinfected with wet wipes, which must be disposed of correctly.

4. Any open wounds you have sustained, such as cuts or scrapes, should be tended to with great care. Make use of waterproof dressings or drapes around open wounds to control radioactivity distribution and rinse them out with clean water regularly.

The proper management and disposal of radioactive waste is very important to decrease the risk of exposure for other people in your family or group. It only takes one of you to bring it into the shelter and it compromises everyone.

When handling hazardous material, keep it inside containers designed for radiation containment with tight seals so nothing can get out or contaminate anything else. These kinds of containers are examples of important items that you will want to stockpile for a nuclear catastrophe just like storing food and water.

Label each container with what's inside along with its level of radioactivity for recognition purposes, if known. The waste should be retained at a location until the radiation decays sufficiently so you can dispose it offsite like any other refuse or until an adequate amount accumulates for careful and proper disposal. Always make sure that any waste is disposed of at least two hundred feet away from your shelter and the nearest water source. In other words, don't dump radioactive water into the nearest source of clean water or you're probably going to die. One feels that this shouldn't be necessary to say, but people on TikTok are eating 500 grams of butter in their dinner nowadays, so you can't take anything for granted.

Finally, to minimize the danger of contamination, clean all surfaces and objects that have been exposed to radiation or fallout in your shelter regularly. This should be a part of your daily ritual when you wake up in the morning and before you go to bed at night, you dirty pig.

With the clothes disposed of and the people cleaned, you can feel more confident that radiation is being kept at bay. Ultimately, you don't want to have to deal with so much radiation on your own for long, but with any luck government help will be on the way to assist you in leaving the area.

CHAPTER TEN:

HOW TO TREAT RADIATION EXPOSURE

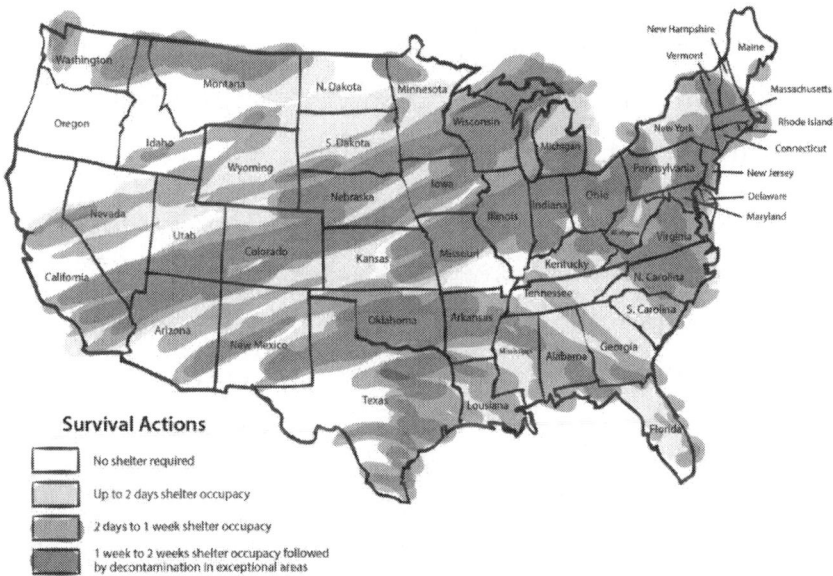

Survival Actions

- No shelter required
- Up to 2 days shelter occupancy
- 2 days to 1 week shelter occupancy
- 1 week to 2 weeks shelter occupancy followed by decontamination in exceptional areas

So, if someone has been a right silly sausage and hasn't followed the tips laid out in Chapter Nine and they've become exposed to radiation, what to do? It's quite possible that you're reading this chapter as a reference for what to do, so you should probably skip through this inane babble at the start and read the next paragraphs. It should be clear that radiation is one of the biggest dangers you will face in the aftermath of a nuclear attack, being aware of how to treat exposure is important.

Knowing what steps to take as soon as possible can literally mean life-or-death in this scenario. This includes understanding radiation sources and how to avoid them as explored in previous chapters. But how do you treat it when you or a family member has been exposed?

Radiation can be emitted from a variety of sources, such as nuclear explosions, accidental occurrences, or contact with radioactive materials through food, water, or skin. The intensity and duration of radiation sickness depend largely on the level of radiation received during an atomic incident or emergency.

Chronic doses over time may lead to health complications including thyroid cancer and accelerated aging. These are prolonged exposures at lower levels than those immediately associated with disaster scenarios like radiological/nuclear emergencies.

As you'll learn in this chapter, determining dose and periodicity are critical elements for understanding potential risks related to dealing with this invisible danger.

****

It's important to know how to protect yourself from radiation exposure, not only in the event of a nuclear blast. Radiation exposure can also arise from accidents involving radioactivity or contact with radioactive substances. It may result in an acute case of radiation sickness appearing shortly after the incident or possibly develop as a chronic illness over time, sometimes years later. Symptoms related to this type of ionizing radiation exposure occur gradually and increase according to the intensity (or dose) and length (duration) of that same radioactive event.

When radiation exposure occurs, the bone marrow, gastrointestinal tract, and skin may be some of the first to show symptoms. At lower levels, there might be muscle aches as well as a metallic taste in one's mouth. Fever and confusion are other symptoms in mild cases. Higher doses can cause nausea, vomiting, or diarrhea, which are signs of radiation sickness. Other more serious signs are hair loss, internal bleeding, or harm caused to the central nervous system due to the higher doses of radiation involved. If you spot these serious symptoms, take them seriously. Of course, you should always take these symptoms seriously, no one should be saying "oh you're losing your hair and vomiting? Tuesdays, am I right?!" But in a post-nuclear bomb world, be double cautious.

Ongoing radiation sickness is potentially deadly and can be caused by exposure to over 400 roentgens or 4 gray (Gy) of radiation. If left untreated, it can result in organ failure or death within 30 days. Severe cases may lead to a coma. It is crucial that anyone exposed to this amount of radiation get medical attention right away to prevent any long-term consequences.

It's worth repeating that the first step to protect against the worsening of any of these symptoms is to take swift action to put distance between yourself and the exposure source. This can help reduce levels of radioactive absorption by the body. Further, the decontamination processes described in the previous chapter should be carried out to remove external particles that may contain radioactivity as well as stop contamination from spreading within a given environment. Should these steps be taken correctly, then there is potential for avoiding acute radiation syndrome or other health conditions stemming from long-term exposure down the line.

Administering first aid for injuries related to these events if crucial and could be lifesaving. Using potassium iodide (KI) to help reduce exposure risks from radioactive particles in iodine-rich areas is your first port of call.

The use of potassium iodide can protect against thyroid cancer in those exposed to radiation. It does this by blocking the absorption of radioactive iodine into the gland, thus minimizing long-term damage resulting from exposure. This should only be done under a doctor's supervision or upon instructions given by local emergency personnel for maximum effectiveness and safety. If used properly, potassium iodide helps reduce threats posed to thyroid health due to contact with radioactivity. Note that protection only applies to the thyroid with no benefits toward other organs or specific types of radioactivity.

****

When facing significant radiation exposure, healthcare decision-making is greatly facilitated when you understand the available medical treatments. These encompass supportive care, bone marrow therapy for regeneration and restoration of cells impacted by radiation damage, radiotherapy to alleviate symptoms caused by intense levels of radiation exposure as well as managing internal contamination through elimination or containment techniques. Disease control measures may also be employed so you have a better fighting chance against any long-lasting effects resulting from this kind of exposure with regard to radioactivity.

Supportive care for radiation exposure is vital in mitigating its physical and emotional effects. To manage symptoms such as nausea, vomiting, and diarrhea while providing relief from pain, patients may receive medication. Neupogen (a drug that encourages the development of white blood cells) can help guard against infection. Nplate, on the other hand, stimulates platelet production to reduce bleeding associated with radiation contact.

When exposed to radiation, and if you're lucky enough to still have access to ongoing professional medical treatment, you can look into treatments like protein medications and blood transfusions that may help reduce the effects of radiation sickness on bone marrow. More severe cases might require a stem cell transplant to restore the production of essential red and white blood cells as well as restoring damage caused by exposure. Research is underway examining the potential benefits of undergoing an actual bone marrow transplant for those affected by such afflictions due to radiation exposure.

Other treatments exist like Prussian blue and Diethylenetriamine Pentaacetic Acid (DTPA). Prussian blue is a medication that binds to radioactive substances in the body and aids their removal from within. DTPA also helps remove contaminated particles but has potential side effects as it ties up essential minerals such as zinc, magnesium, or manganese found inside our bodies. Awareness regarding these treatments enables us to handle situations involving radiation with greater confidence should we ever find ourselves exposed to hazardous levels of radioactivity due to any chance incident.

You may, by now, be realizing that radiation exposure is serious and not something you can put a band-aid over and ignore. Real, proper doctors are needed to help save lives here, but knowing what treatments are possible will help direct you, even if the world is in crisis and there's little help available.

****

While there are treatments available, it should be reiterated that prevention is the best approach when it comes to radiation exposure. Those working in potentially hazardous environments should always comply with security standards as well as use protective gear when confronted by any type of irradiation.

In terms of the average person's ability to deal with a nuclear event, having an organized action plan, complete with evacuation routes and communications protocols in place, is the best approach to protect against the damaging effects of radiation on yourself, your family, and your surrounding communities.

CHAPTER ELEVEN:

HOW LONG SHOULD YOU STAY IN SHELTER AFTER A NUCLEAR FALLOUT?

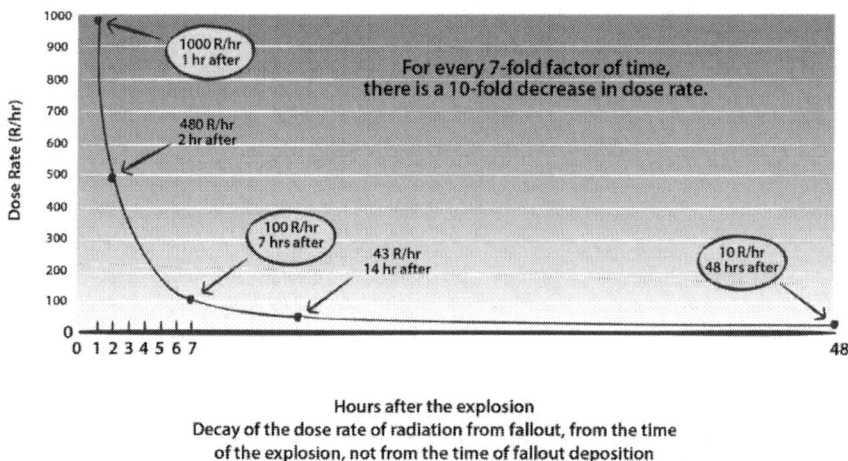

1000 R/hr
1 hr after

For every 7-fold factor of time, there is a 10-fold decrease in dose rate.

480 R/hr
2 hr after

100 R/hr
7 hrs after

43 R/hr
14 hr after

10 R/hr
48 hrs after

Hours after the explosion
Decay of the dose rate of radiation from fallout, from the time
of the explosion, not from the time of fallout deposition

Much like with a late-night curry, the lingering effects of a nuclear bomb can be serious and the cause of misery and disease. It is essential to enter an enclosed structure and remain there until directions are received from emergency response teams in order to avoid radiation after a bomb has struck.

Radiation levels tend to reduce quickly within twenty-four hours, in some situations however, it could take nearly one month for radioactivity values to drop enough that an environment can be considered safe. In other scenarios, up to five years might be needed for the rates of exposure to not be risky anymore; in those cases, people would be evacuated on a more permanent basis.

In the event of a nuclear attack, you must act quickly. A Wireless Emergency Alert (WEA) text on your cell phone can be used to notify that a nuclear strike or similar attack is incoming, and it is necessary to seek shelter without delay in any nearby building while avoiding contact with windows as we covered previously in this book. All mobile phones will be contacted, so make sure you don't use up all your battery swiping left and right on post-apocalyptic Tinder.

When you have knowledge or reason to believe that a nuclear strike is about to happen in your area, get as far away as possible as quickly as you can! If you have a shelter away from an urbanized area like we've covered repeatedly in this book as well, work on getting you and your family to that shelter as fast as you possibly can.

****

Once you've followed the advice provided in previous chapters regarding what to do immediately following a nuclear event and in the immediate aftermath regarding shelter and evacuation, you might be wondering, "What next?"

The key to devising your next steps is to monitor radiation levels. This will help you know when you can safely emerge from your shelter. Radiation exposure reduces by 55% an hour after the blast and 80% over 24 hours. Within three days, it will decrease by 90%, and within two weeks, it will decrease by 99%. There should be a noticeable decrease in these readings within three days. Wait *at least* 24 hours before leaving your shelter, but taking longer and waiting three days as we've discussed further would be even better. Think about it like a bottle of wine, the longer you leave it, the better it will be.

This effectively demonstrates why time limitation is imperative when attempting to protect yourself from nuclear radiation hazards: simply reduce or eliminate your radiation exposure, and the chances of you becoming infected with the radiation will drop significantly. It really is that simple.

When it's time to venture out, either to evacuate or gather resources, pay attention to any additional instructions given by local authorities. Emergency response officials will provide the guidelines to be followed so people can know if it is safe enough to leave their shelter. The instructions of authorities must always be strictly obeyed, and individuals could even have to go to another nuclear fallout shelter designated by them depending on the situation.

When you finally venture outside, make sure that your entire body is covered. Wear a hazmat suit, have boots, wear gloves, and have goggles around your eyes while making sure that your head and face are completely covered. Make sure that there are no rips or holes in your clothing (or openings in the seams) that could allow radiation to seep through.

You should also use your own monitoring to recognize radioactive zones as well as safe paths away from them. To accurately gauge radiation levels, access equipment such as Geiger counters. Those unfamiliar with their operation will need advice from experienced professionals, so consider learning how to use these devices now. Experienced professionals, by the way, doesn't mean someone on TikTok. Find someone who knows the equipment well to show you in person. You never want the aftermath of an actual nuclear strike to be the first time you're using these devices.

****

The desire to connect with others (such as your friends and family members) is the most likely motivator that will prematurely drive you out of your shelter before it is safe to do so. So, to be prepared for a nuclear emergency, an effective plan should include the ability to communicate with others. This is for peace of mind, and with vital information to help you stay safe.

The necessary steps in creating your Family Emergency Communications Plan are: (1) finding someone outside of your area who can serve as a contact person (and having the ability to contact them via a CB radio or HAM radio since internet and cell service will be down); (2) teaching all family members about this;

(3) making sure that everybody is familiar with the plan and how to connect if needed. Having contact with the outside world will reassure you and help you to stay safely inside your shelter.

For some people, no doubt, the cut off of communication will be a blessed relief, however. So, if you're one of those people, please enjoy your quiet few days away from family members and take the time to catch up on those books you've not been reading.

****

If you have been forced to evacuate by the authorities before the nuclear blast went off, follow emergency response officials' instructions and only return to your home when told it is safe to do so by local authorities. Remember that recovery from a nuclear bomb will likely take up to ten years in total, though long-term global changes cannot be ruled out. The reduced ozone concentrations may also have further consequences for areas outside of the direct detonation sites.

The 7:10 Rule of Thumb is a way to calculate the expected future radiation exposure rate based on measurements taken shortly after detonation. This rule states that as time goes by, there will be an approximate 10-fold decrease for every seven-fold increase in the elapsed period since the explosion.

For maximum protection against radiation during a nuclear fallout, seek shelter in an underground brick or concrete building for a minimum of twenty-four hours after the event and then re-evaluate with the guidance of local authorities and radiation monitoring devices.

CHAPTER TWELVE:

SURVIVING FROM TWENTY-FOUR TO SEVENTY-TWO HOURS FOLLOWING A NUCLEAR ATTACK

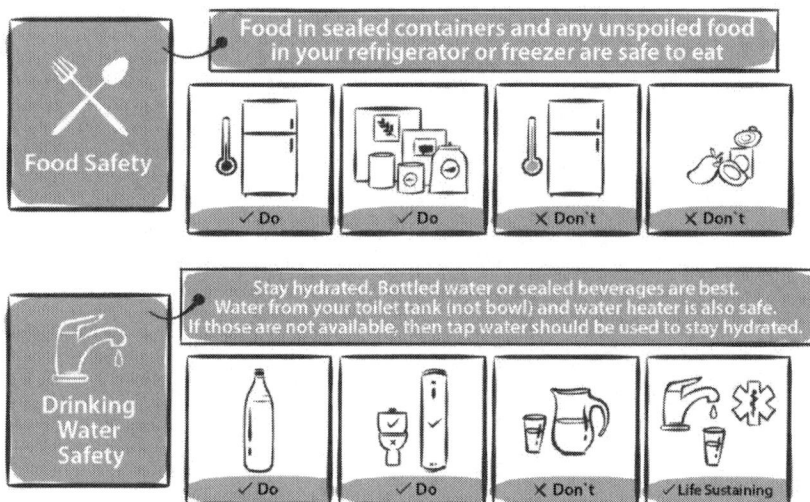

In this chapter, we'll dive into providing you with essential information and tips that can help ensure survival during the crucial 24 to 72-hour window post-nuclear incident. As we've discussed previously in this book, this period is crucial because it's the period in which leftover radiation will begin to dissipate at a faster rate. By approximately the 72-hour mark following a nuclear explosion, around 90% of the nuclear radiation will have (at least in normal circumstances) gone away.

Furthermore, experts often point out how your chances of surviving the first 72 hours following any kind of disaster will greatly increase your odds of survival over the long term. That's because, in most disaster scenarios, the most danger occurs within the initial 72-hour window. After all, that's when most of the chaos following a disaster ensues as people chaotically try to adapt to the rapidly changed circumstances. Surviving after the first 72-hour period doesn't guarantee your survival over the long term, but it should increase your odds. Much like a bachelor party.

We'll cover preparation strategies for this period that could mean the difference between life and death. To ensure that you have the best chance of surviving these 72 hours, you'll need to continue to stay informed, manage your resources, monitor for changes in radiation levels, continue to treat injuries, begin to address any mental health concerns and plan for the future. These initiatives can help minimize the danger posed by any type of nuclear threat and keep those around you secure during this crucial phase.

****

During the most catastrophic events, it may take up to seventy-two hours for broadcasts to begin or for you to establish a connection. Keeping up to date with news reports will provide critical information when choosing protective measures during this high-pressure timeframe. By seeking this information, you can remain in touch with the advice being offered by government agencies and experts in the know about the big picture. Cell phones or radios that can access the emergency broadcast network may give you access to key details to help you make informed decisions. That being said, in the event of a severe enough nuclear blast (or blasts) that knocks out all of the power across the United States (or in whichever country you live in), then chances are very strong that electronic communication along with the news will remain offline..., and for a very extended period.

Furthermore, during the 72-hour window (and beyond) you won't be able to rely on the authorities to save you, even if a connection to the news and the outside world is established. During this period, it's important to monitor your resources to ensure efficient use and to extend the lifespan of supplies. Restricting how much of each resource can be used per day, along with ensuring they are only employed when essential, will give you an effective way of rationing food, water, and medical necessities. This careful handling of provisions guarantees availability beyond these critical first days. Decisions you make about resources during this time could prove impactful, particularly if you encounter problems sourcing items later.

Consider rationing your water usage to only a half gallon of water per person per day. This will ensure that each person drinks enough water to remain at least somewhat hydrated, while hopefully making your water supply last for as long as possible. Ultimately, however, how you ration your food, water, and other resources comes down to factors such as how much you have on hand and how many people you have to take care of. Plan appropriately. If you have it in mind that you're preparing for a marathon, not a sprint, you'll be well served.

Monitoring radiation exposure is another critical part of keeping your family safe. As mentioned, devices such as Geiger counters can be used to measure the levels present in an area and advise if it's advisable to leave your shelter or not. This is something you need to do continuously beyond the first twenty fur hours. To get comprehensive data, emergency management may also deploy aerial surveys, ground scans plus specialized detectors for more detailed assessments before allowing those sheltered back out into the environment safely. Staying updated on all current radiation information increases your protection against any potential hazards that come from direct exposure.

To reduce radiation exposure and maintain health, it is important to stay away from areas that are potentially contaminated. During this phase of the crisis, you may start to be more mobile around your local area or even have to travel some distance to evacuate. Areas near the blast site or in a downwind direction have likely been greatly affected by the nuclear fallout. If there's any indication of contamination (such as a non-ordinary smell or glow), you should quickly move out of this area. By doing so, you can lessen your chances of being exposed to unsafe levels of radiation brought on by a nuclear attack and protect yourself against possible sickness due to these particles. Imagine yourself at a party, where someone has knocked the lavatory out of commission with a stinky missile of their own. You'll want to move away from it to avoid the effects, and ideally to remove yourself from association or being misattributed as its owner. It's roughly the same sort of thing as nuclear bombs.

****

In this post-nuclear attack period, concern for your health and safety and those of your loved ones must remain the utmost priority, though ideally that should always be the concern. Understanding how to address potential injuries, steer clear of radiation sickness, and maintain mental wellness are all extremely important considerations. The aim is to ensure the best possible outcome during this critical span of 72 hours following a nuclear attack. Sustaining your overall wellbeing through such an alarming ordeal will give you the best chance for successful survival in the wake of a destructive episode like this one.

The aftermath of a nuclear event will become a volatile and extremely chaotic situation. As a result, you will need to use hiding strategies and self-defense methods that can help guarantee your survival. You must consider the fact that the post-nuclear world might be lawless and a place of anarchy, with violence and rioting due to limited resources being a real threat. Armed raiding parties and looters will take to the streets (at least whichever streets are left) and forcefully take whatever supplies they can find with the use of violence if they have to. Desperate people will do desperate things in desperate times, including once-normal people who had never hurt anyone in their old lives. We've all seen footage of Black Friday, haven't we? We know how bad it can get when (discounted) resources are thin.

This is why a good strategy right from the beginning to the end of a nuclear blast is to keep it out of sight of anyone else. Adopting the "gray man" approach can help you blend into your surroundings and go unnoticed. This means you should dress in dull colors that 'blend in' with the surrounding environment, as well as clothing that is not attention-grabbing. Speak softly and avoid eye contact with others so that you remain inconspicuous. If you find yourself in a crowd of people, move in the direction of the crowd rather than against it. Your survival chances will be much higher if you proactively take steps to disappear.

Being proficient in self-defense strategies is key to staying safe from potential risks. Martial arts can provide an efficient way of defending yourself against such threats. Don't learn this yourself, however, start going to classes or you'll be rubbish at it. Improved physical and mental fitness will also assist you in dealing with radioactive contamination removal successfully. Basic techniques like blocking, eluding, or escaping may prove useful when trying to protect yourself against possible dangers stemming from hazardous materials including radioactivity. Adopting the correct posture, which consists of raising your heel and bringing both of your arms up for defense, could go a long way toward keeping you safe and secure.

Look and watch for information about threats like radiation and raiding parties in your region. Make use of news sources, social media platforms, and emergency warning systems to remain informed. When formulating your defense plan, take into account all factors: the size of your home, the occupants present, and the available resources. Consider crafting an alternate option should primary security measures fail.

As we addressed previously in this book as well, the way you construct and locate your shelter should consider this aspect of the post-nuclear environment as well. A secure space is paramount. Conceal the location well, make it difficult to access by others, stock up on essential items like food and water, and strengthen entrance points with locks and other security features.

To mislead anyone intent on raiding your home, keep lights off inside and open windows outside while placing broken objects around the house to create an impression of abandonment. Reinforce doors/windows using metal bars or grates along with installing motion-sensors and alarms plus establishing lookouts.

This way you'll be aware of any potential intruders attempting entry into your safe haven. Always have an escape plan just in case!

Proactively acquiring useful knowledge along with maximizing readiness can arm you against the volatile environment after a nuclear attack.

****

Long-term survival plans are critical to successfully navigating a post-nuclear attack. You'll need tactics that involve resilience, ingenuity, and creativity to endure new struggles as well as providing mutual help during difficult times. Having long-term strategies in mind is essential when adapting to nuclear fallout. This approach can ensure the greatest possible benefit both individually and at a community level. This 24-to-72-hour period is the time to begin making such plans.

Living in a post-apocalyptic environment comes with its own difficulties. While protecting yourself as described above is important, you must also develop resilience strategies to help rebuild communities. This means becoming resourceful and inventive to create new ways of life together while offering support for each other under challenging conditions. Doing so will benefit everyone's survival prospects greatly.

CHAPTER THIRTEEN:

FINDING FOOD AND WATER AFTER NUCLEAR WAR

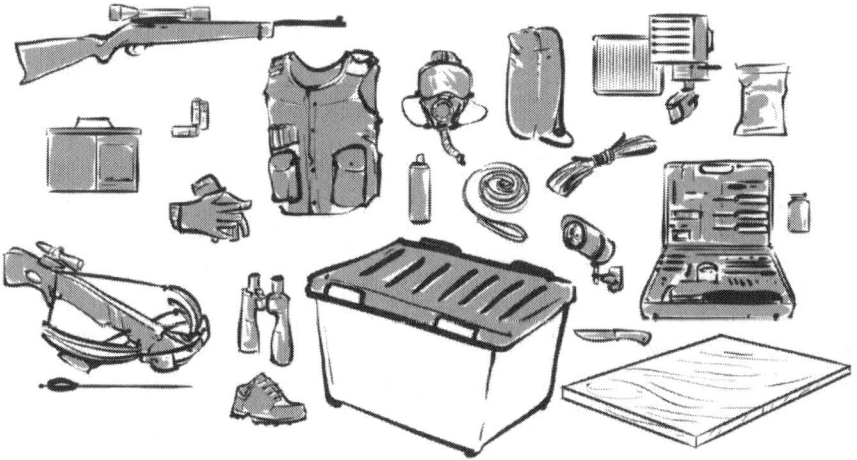

In the face of a new world impacted by nuclear war, your survival will be based on your ability to find food sources, purify water, and protect your existing food and water sources. Your approach in this new environment must also consider the potential risks that are associated with contaminated resources. These measures are key for living through the long-term effects of a nuclear war where finding new food sources will be immensely difficult. You won't be able to survive on dried noodles and Snickers bars forever you know.

Secure procedures must be put in place to reduce the risk posed by nuclear war. Connecting sites with such hazardous substances brings risks, including radioactive fallout spreading past the detonation site, pollution of food and water supplies, as well as long-term health impacts Radioactive materials like cesium-137 and strontium-90 will possess lingering effects that can reach not only humans but also domestic animals too. Complications regarding access to safe food sources may arise because of this occurrence.

To prepare for this, you need an understanding of the primary threats that will arise in a post-nuclear war world during your search to find food: contamination from isotopes could cause radiation sickness, cancers, and mutations in genes (those of both plants and people).

The extensive, long-term health repercussions of a nuclear war could adversely affect several future generations to come. Radiation sickness, cancer, and genetic changes are all possible effects of contact with radioactive fallout. To these dangers, the force generated by an atomic explosion can cause considerable destruction as well. A huge cloud filled with radiation released after such blasts carry radionuclides that have been known to spread over vast spaces, which increases the chances of exposure for many people.

Many survivors may suffer from cancers affecting areas like the lungs or gastrointestinal system. Female breast cancer has also seen spikes due to this same form of contamination following encounters involving nuclear weapons usage. Receiving medical assistance quickly is essential in cases where very large doses of hazardous levels of radioactivity were endured. Surviving becomes extremely unlikely if not treated on time. Taking appropriate measures so you do not come into contact with contaminated food and water is paramount to avert prolonged adverse effects.

****

In a situation of nuclear war, locating safe sources of food is vital to your survival. You'll need to avoid any contaminated food and water sources, as they may bring about severe health consequences. To reduce exposure to radioactive materials, store food in sealed containers or pre-packaged foods that have not been exposed. Examine the expiration dates as well as check for discoloration or odd odors to ensure safety when selecting from these foods. Always replace your stored foods once they have reached their respective expiration dates so they will last for as long as possible once a nuclear incident has occurred.

Avoid including fresh fruits, vegetables, and eggs as part of your long-term food storage survival plan, as they all could carry dangerous levels of radioactivity. For example, mushrooms should be avoided since boiling water would likely fail to eliminate the presence of dangerous substances from them, to make them safe enough to be eaten afterwards. Also make sure you avoid apricot. Not for any particular reason, it's just that it's revolting, and no one will thank you for it.

In the aftermath of a nuclear war, sealed containers like cans and plastic-wrapped foods will become treasure troves as they will offer uncontaminated sources of nourishment. Wipe off any fallout dust on these packages before opening them to guarantee that their food content has not been exposed to radioactive materials, thereby ensuring safety for those consuming it. Containers can provide reliable protection from potential contamination by shielding the food inside from radiation or other hazardous substances that may be present in such post-apocalyptic settings. Consider wiping down food containers and jars with warm water and soap to help wipe away any possible radiation as well. The apocalypse may well be sponsored by Heinz at this rate.

Following a nuclear war, packaged foods will offer several advantages such as sustenance. They have been produced before the event and thus are less likely to be contaminated by radioactive materials. Their shelf life is extended. Plus, they offer convenience, portability, and vital nutrition.

To ensure that these foods remain safe for consumption, wash your hands before handling them (to limit any contamination) then thoroughly cook them once again as an added measure of safety following the nuclear conflict. By taking such precautions when consuming prepackaged food sources, you can guard against ingesting anything potentially hazardous due to radiation exposure incurred during or after said disaster scenario.

Since contamination can linger in the environment for some time, you must give safe sources of sustenance (namely sealed containers or packaged foods) attention during times like this. Remember, avoid fruits, vegetables, eggs, and uncooked fresh meat as they may contain pathogens due to potential contamination.

****

Your ability to survive during a nuclear war is also dependent on locating and purifying an adequate source of water. You should make use of high-grade water sources, such as reservoirs, for collecting drinking water after the attack. Nevertheless, even without a reservoir source, it's still possible to have clean water despite a hazardous situation with proper planning and creative approaches.

Bottled water will be one of the safest means of hydration post-nuclear conflict since it comes packaged securely, preventing contamination from entering it easily. If bottled water supplies are unavailable, don't remain dehydrated but take recourse in drinking possibly contaminated liquid instead, but make sure that you treat it first.

For potentially contaminated water to become consumable, you should conduct various treatments so that radioactive particles may no longer pose any danger. These include filtration or distillation, just as people usually do before drinking other unsafe beverages even without disasters occurring around them.

After any nuclear incident, you should look into bottled water as your primary source of hydration due to its packaging and preparation. There is less of a chance that it will have been affected by contamination or other harmful substances. It also has a convenient form for both transportation and storage. Choosing bottled water can drastically reduce the risks associated with using unsterilized sources, allowing you to stay healthy even after such an event occurs.

You must also take safety measures when washing food with tap water due to potential contamination. The use of proper purification processes such as distillation and filtration should be employed to make sure that drinking or cooking purposes can be safely carried out without any health hazards from radioactive particles. All of these steps must be taken.

You can use various methods of purification to make sure your water is safe to drink, such as distillation, reverse osmosis, clay earth filtration, and ion-exchange filters. This will effectively remove any radioactive particles from the water supply so that it is more fit for drinking. Distillation simply entails boiling the water, which produces steam separate from the contaminants left behind in its original jar. The steam will then turn into condensation to provide you with safe drinking water.

****

Last but certainly not least, you'll also need to take steps to protect your crops and livestock to maintain a safe food supply (if you have any, that is). For crops and plants, this can be done by using greenhouses, which shield plants from radiation as well as providing an environment for growth. For animals, consider moving them indoors so that they are not exposed to the hazards of radioactive particles (if you have the space).

CHAPTER FOURTEEN:

BUILDING COMMUNITY IN THE AFTERMATH OF A NUCLEAR WAR

COMMUNITY
Preparedness
Cycle

(Plan, Organize, Train, Exercise, Evaluate)

In the aftermath of a nuclear war, forming or taking part in solid and resilient communities is an overlooked and yet necessary aspect for the survival of people in your area and human civilization to rebuild as a whole. In this chapter, we will dive into how to survive such an event by taking into consideration urgent survival needs such as shelter, nutrition, and health care.

You may even be able to take the opportunity to remove the music of Drake from human history while you're at it.

The initial moments following a nuclear detonation will pose some very hard challenges that must be immediately addressed. Remember it's the first 72 hours that will always be the toughest to survive. But you've got to make it out alive, find safe refuge, and meet everyone's most basic needs without neglecting any injuries suffered. After these steps have been taken toward immediate relief efforts, survivors will need to go further. They'll need to develop effective ways of communication with each other, handle radiation-related issues associated with the devastation, revive agriculture production after destruction, and build strong bonds between neighbors to ultimately reconstruct community life post-nuclear warfare. All this must be achieved while preserving information safely yet accessible for future generations along the journey toward recovery. It's a lot!

****

The horrendous destruction caused by nuclear weapons is undisputed, and hopefully, that's clear in this book. But one of the overlooked effects of a nuclear blast is the power it has in potentially unleashing a series of violent reactions in people and their environment. Consequently, it's paramount to be prepared for the aftermath following such an explosion, which could prove deadly as people start to turn on one another for supplies and resources. Complicating your survival will likely be the realities of societal collapse.

Do not adopt the lone wolf mentality of thinking that either you or your family can simply survive alone. To survive a post-nuclear war world over the long term, you must coordinate your efforts together with allies by pooling resources together while rationing available stocks. By banding together with other survivors, you will ensure that survival efforts like water collection through rainwater harvesting and gathering sustenance through hunting/foraging will become a lot easier. Living like a hippy commune will serve you well, but there's no pre-requisite of having to listen to lots of 1960s psychedelic music, nor avoiding washing your hair.

There are many aspects to be considered regarding survival following a nuclear war that will be downright impossible without the assistance or help of other people. For instance, it's simply unrealistic to think that you can turn to a hospital or medical clinic to receive medical assistance in the event of you sustaining a serious medical injury. But by working together with a community of like-minded people, you may have someone in your group who is either a medical professional or at least has knowledge or experience in first aid and can provide assistance.

Ultimately, everyone in a group of people will have different talents and skill sets, each of which can be used collectively to increase the chances of survival for everyone in the group as a whole. This is precisely why survivors following a nuclear event must act quickly on their own behalf and also on behalf of one another. You don't know how long your new community will need to survive, it could be a matter of days, or it could extend to months depending on the destruction.

This is also why you should try to form a community of like-minded people *before* a nuclear strike (or any other major disaster for that matter) occurs. Once a disaster has occurred, you can band together following the initial 72-hour period where the contamination outside will be strongest. Make sure that you have a way to communicate with each person in your group, such as with HAM or CB radios, and also make sure that every person has the right attire to ensure that every part of their body is protected against nuclear radiation.

Remember that the aftermath of a nuclear war has the potential to destroy communication systems and infrastructure due to an electromagnetic pulse going off. Re-establishing communications as well as fostering trust between survivors is essential for them to coordinate their efforts, distribute information, and ask for outside help. This involves rebuilding affected communication networks, but also inspiring confidence among those who survived so that they are willing to work together.

After a nuclear war, the critical task of restoring communication systems is essential to share vital information and coordinate actions. Reconstructing an effective command network requires designing a framework that can remain stable despite the damage to infrastructure while providing secure and reliable links between leaders.

It will take some time until networks are operational again after such a disaster, so taking advantage of every kind of technology available (such as radios, satellite phones, or other quick solutions) and not giving up when trying to reestablish connections will make all the difference. One must also remember that our previous technology and devices may not work after an event. Don't be sat around attempting to slide into someone's DMs on Instagram, you'll have to try other methods first.

After a nuclear war, survivors need to develop trust and collaboration to rebuild their lives. To achieve this, all parties must be provided with equitable resources and assistance, as well as cooperating on matters of importance. It is also important to set fair guidelines that recognize the needs of everyone while creating an atmosphere encouraging collective effort. When people come together collaboratively, they have the chance not only to reconstruct their communities but to build unity among them too.

****

It's essential in a post-nuclear blast that contamination levels be monitored and evaluated so appropriate steps can be taken, including establishing exclusion zones around contaminated areas with restricted access, applying cleaning techniques like eliminating dirtied soil or vegetation and handling polluted water sources properly. Other steps that you must take include making sure radiation doesn't spread by, for instance, covering exposed surfaces or closing off buildings; disposing of

133

radioactivity-infused waste safely; and closely keeping track of radiation amounts to make certain safety persists going forward. All these measures would need to be implemented to ensure people living nearby receive proper protection from harmful effects connected to the nuclear incident and to do these steps effectively, you'll need multiple people handling each one as well.

Your community can utilize radiation detectors and dosimeters for measuring radiation levels. This will enable you to make decisions concerning sheltering, evacuation, or resource management. To prevent contact with such material, proper protective garments have to be worn as well as appropriate safety equipment when dealing with contaminated items. Education about the danger of exposure must also take place so individuals are aware of how they should get around these hazardous substances. This requires leadership and consensus-building among the community and is another reason why it's important to put a community together before any disaster strikes so you can ensure that everyone in the group is properly educated about the steps that will need to be taken following a nuclear event. Make sure that arguments and conflict are dealt with quickly and fairly, the last thing your community needs in the apocalypse is a fight breaking out over who gets to paint their shelter orange or who had the deck of cards last.

****

The destructive impacts of a nuclear conflict on agricultural food supplies could be catastrophic for survivors. There is potential for famine and severe hunger due to reduced temperatures, radiation-caused reduction in production rates, as well as changes in precipitation affecting the growth rate of certain crops.

To efficiently adapt to various modifications in our eco-systems, measures such as crop diversification, utilization of sustainable farming practices, an introduction of new species would need to be taken. In light of the limited resources and complex environmental conditions encountered during this process, innovating ideas and collective work will be of great value.

Trying out unconventional agricultural approaches like hydroponic cultivation or vertical agriculture is a great way to enhance food production faced with varied ecosystems. Working together by exchanging essential knowledge and experiences can turn into an unbeatable strategy for adjusting peacefully while reconstructing at the same time. (Again, buy a book on small-scale or at home agricultural methods to help prepare for this.)

Rebuilding local economies after a nuclear war is critical to the survival of affected communities. This can be accomplished by providing employment opportunities, increasing access to capital, and promoting entrepreneurship through small businesses. Training courses and investment in local industries will be essential for creating sustainable livelihoods that give survivors financial stability long-term.

To effectively carry out this task, it is important to collaborate with neighboring areas so resources may be pooled together more efficiently. Exchanging information about expertise will also aid in achieving economic recovery faster than if each community went alone - building resilience for future generations across multiple regions at once.

****

Forming communities in the aftermath of a nuclear war is necessary to ensure that people in general will have access to resources, resilience, and optimism. Together, people can help restore one another's homes or provide refuge to others while providing each other with essential food and water supplies as well.

Through this community support structure, trust develops, which allows everyone's needs to be taken into account effectively, fostering unity within the group affected by disaster. Community building after a nuclear blast will help strengthen hope amongst the victims, especially in an era where PTSD and shock will set in quickly for most people. This gives people a reason to survive despite the great loss suffered from the destruction caused by the nuclear incident. Working together as part of a community will help give people new goals that are not just about themselves but about other people as well, and having goals in this manner that are a part of the 'common good' will be one of the best strategies people can use to help mitigate the effects of the shock and PTSD that they will feel.

A reliable system of resource-sharing is key to promoting harmony among all members of the community. To give everyone a safeguard and induce solidarity, you can use an aid network that offers food, water, and medical supplies to all within your group and within reason The administration for this aid network must take age, health status, and family size into consideration when establishing fair distribution methods between survivors. By combining resources and working in tandem toward this goal, your chances at long-term survival will become better all while creating a more cohesive unit within the group.

CHAPTER FIFTEEN:

HOW TO LIVE FOR THE LONG TERM IN A POST-NUCLEAR WAR WORLD

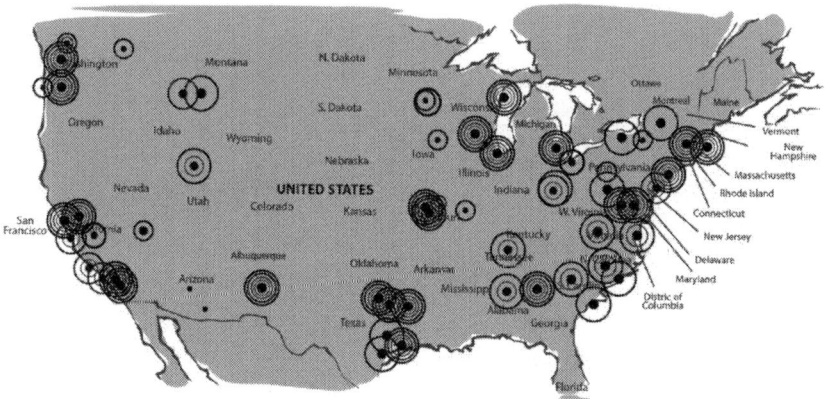

If a nuclear strike happens, you and the other survivors in your group will need to find ways to survive and adapt to this new world. There will be no alternative. As we discussed before, the days of going to the grocery store, setting aside money to take a nice vacation sometime in the year, and driving into the office to work each day will no longer be a reality. Instead, every single moment will become about the steps you and the other members of your group can take to survive. There is some opportunity that comes with this, you can make the world what you want it to be, despite the immense difficulties ahead.

In this chapter, we will explore the various strategies that you can use for long-term survival following such an event by looking at history, fictional tales, and scientific research on the subject. The challenge will be to figure out how to make it through these dark times while ensuring our safety despite all the destruction caused by a nuclear war.

****

In the event of a nuclear attack, survivors must be prepared with a safe and secure shelter to protect against direct radiation, blast waves, and fallout.

Sustainable energy sources should be employed within the shelter like solar power, wind power, geothermal power, or hydropower so vital resources remain operational even after disaster strikes. Other essentials include food supplies along with water supply systems plus medical items set aside alongside proper waste disposal plans for sanitation reasons where applicable. By following these guidelines, you can expect to shelter safely for a minimum of the 72-hour period that we've been discussing.

In the wake of a nuclear war, mastering essential skills is key for ensuring human survival. You can get a head-start on these as part of your preparations. First aid knowledge can assist with wound treatment, resuscitation techniques and use of medical equipment while farming entails expertise in soil preparation and animal husbandry alongside crop rotation. Expert hunting abilities are also needed to find food and building sources which will then help people construct shelters as well as energy systems through basic engineering skills that they must develop. Cookery and baking will be helpful as well. Very little boosts the soul as much as a sandwich, so learn how to make a good loaf of bread and your community will value you immensely. Such skills would allow survivors to effectively manage any kind of injury or illness while supporting civilization's rebuilding efforts along the way - enabling them to remain resilient within their post-nuclear world landscape and secure future security throughout humankind's existence too.

****

In the event of a full-scale global nuclear war, the human population must understand and adjust to enormous changes in climate that may come as a result. These possible environmental consequences could include firestorms or an intensely cold winter. The latter would be due to radiation exposure from multiple nuclear explosions during a nuclear exchange involving existing weapons on both sides. Ecosystem disruptions may also occur on an unpredictable yet widespread scale if such drastic measures are taken by two or more countries possessing large numbers of these highly destructive armaments.

The heat of atomic blasts could create huge firestorms and put considerable amounts of soot into our atmosphere. That may result in an "ice age"-like phenomenon where sunlight is blocked out, causing lower temperatures on Earth's surface. This chill would bring with it damaging effects such as global food shortages, and problems for ocean life caused by a reduction in primary production, along with long-term elevated UV rays, creating health risks for those who remain after the catastrophe.

Those left must be up for the challenge because they can no longer rely on their normal resources for survival. People will need creative solutions such as alternate nourishment methods or building secure dwellings that are shielded from harmful ultraviolet radiation levels. Otherwise, humans will be completely wiped off the planet due to these catastrophic circumstances brought about by nuclear warfare.

Survivors of such an event must find ways to cope with this new reality by seeking alternative sources of sustenance while striving toward sustaining their local environment. You'll need to come up with creative solutions to maintain ecological equilibrium in post-nuclear warfare. Be adaptable! Even if you're conservative in politics, be liberal in life.

****

The rebuilding of society and the economy in the aftermath of a nuclear event would be a substantial challenge. Infrastructure damage, depletion of natural resources, as well as widespread population shifts will impede this process significantly. Humans have an incredible capacity for overcoming obstacles by being resilient and adaptive to their environment. Steps toward achieving restoration could include setting up communities, trading goods through bartering systems, promoting education, or honing skills that are necessary along with other prerequisites required to get back on track.

After a nuclear war, the creation of supportive communities will be essential for survivors to cope with such dire circumstances. Cooperation and strong leadership along with effective communication will be integral components. Watch out for power-hungry people, and don't let your new society fall into aggression or fighting. Re-establishing vital infrastructures like housing complexes, sanitary systems as well as communications networks will require collective resources and efforts by all individuals involved. It will be equally important to build up food supply storages plus medical establishments since these amenities are vital for sustaining a sound lifestyle within the new community setup.

To achieve this goal, everyone must have a sense of unity and one shared destiny to foster the ability to surmount any future challenges arising from the post-nuclear mayhem, thus spurring hope out of ruinous despair! Deciding on an identity or core set of beliefs to build upon will help to unify your group, and make sure you're pulling in the same direction.

In a post-apocalyptic landscape, traditional economic systems will no longer exist. As such, bartering and direct exchanges of goods will likely become the primary method for trading. Don't accept dollars, lira, nor euros in any transaction. That bit of paper will do little to help anyone now beyond being used to light a fire! To successfully carry out bartering transactions, trust must be cultivated between those involved and the necessary skills or resources must be present. This can assist survivors with obtaining items not easily accessible otherwise while simultaneously promoting financial recovery throughout society by allowing commodities to be redistributed freely.

Also in a post-nuclear world, education and the mastery of essential skills will become super critical for the survival of future generations. Traditional educational systems will have been greatly affected by this event, necessitating alternative methods for gaining knowledge. These would include first aid, agriculture and hunting techniques, as well as basic engineering strategies - all of these will need to be taught to guarantee the reconstruction of human civilization. Writing or documenting events will also be crucial, helping to provide a history and record of what's happened and what you're doing in the apocalypse. Who knows, your diary might well become a best seller... whenever they start selling things again.

Communication proficiency along with problem-solving abilities are also key. These two capabilities combined with critical thinking plus resource management are essential to the societal regeneration process. By providing everyone living after the nuclear fallout access to substantial education and viable skill development, people will equip themselves to participate in a functional economic landscape once again.

****

The repercussions of a nuclear war would be far-reaching and severely compromise human life. There is an urgent need to take action on all fronts, including in health care, nutrition security, and emotional resilience to safeguard society now against the effects of such a catastrophe. In addition to the immediate harm caused by radiation exposure or environmental degradation, long-term issues surrounding food supplies as well as physical infrastructure must also be considered when looking at possible preparation solutions. Thus, it requires dedication from multiple areas if we are going to look out for our own safety following this kind of destruction.

In a post-nuclear world, the immediate effects of radiation on humans could be debilitating and long-term medical care would face many challenges. First aid skills such as wound treatment or cardiopulmonary resuscitation will have to suffice when it comes to managing these health issues due to a lack of resources and facilities. Providing proper attention for exposure poisoning, preventing infections, and treating any injuries caused by the initial blast is crucial for supporting survivors in their communities.

A plentiful stock of medicinal supplies plus full knowledge about how radiation can impact people are necessary elements needed to provide adequate medical assistance after an attack like this has occurred. By understanding potential risks associated with nuclear fallout and related health-care necessities, survivalists like yourself might properly prepare more thoroughly and guarantee safety within society afterwards.

Food production and supply are key for the health and well-being of people in a post-nuclear world. The disruption to food production, as well as contamination of fresh products, necessitates stockpiling non-perishable items while at the same time relying on alternative sources to meet nutritional needs. To address this issue, survivors should focus their energy on growing and preserving their own food with sustainable agriculture methods.

Water purification measures should be taken alongside proper sanitation practices in order to ensure long-term nutritional security. Emphasizing these precautions will help prevent issues such as malnutrition or disease from occurring amongst communities after experiencing the great upheaval caused by nuclear events.

CHAPTER SIXTEEN:

ADDITIONAL TIPS FOR SURVIVING A NUCLEAR WAR

Sirens blaring and emergency broadcasts interrupting your day-to-day routine may be alarming signals that nuclear war has begun. People would be rushing around, trying desperately to find safety and protect those they care about most deeply.

Our final chapter will cover crucial tips on staying alive in that scenario, which includes covering important topics such as hidden dangers, unconventional tactics for success, community-based protective measures, and new technologies available specifically for surviving this type of disaster, as well as the processes necessary once radiation recedes enough so people can start rebuilding their lives post-tragedy.

ESTIMATED GLOBAL NUCLEAR WARHEAD INVENTORIES, 2023

RUSSIA
5,889 ↗

UNITED
KINGDOM
225 ↗

UNITED STATE
5,244 ↘

NORTH KOREA
30 ↗

FRANCE
290 ⇌

ISRAEL
90 ⇌

CHINA
410 ↗

PAKISTAN
170 ↗

INDIA
164 ↗

↗ Countries with increasing warhead stockpiles:
   China, India, North Korea, Pakistan, Russia, UK

⇌ Countries with stable warhead stockpiles: France, Israel

↘ Countries with decreasing warhead stockpiles: US

Knowing these overlooked tips could mean life or death when it comes down to it. By taking into consideration all possible approaches before something horrific occurs, we set ourselves up better than anyone else for increased chances of overcoming any potential hardship associated with experiencing nuclear war firsthand.

Utilizing Natural Resources

Essential for surviving in a post-nuclear world, natural resources provide the basic needs of life such as food, water, shelter, and energy. These materials are also used to fashion tools and weapons that can defend against various hazards. Examples include water for drinking, cooking, and cleaning; air to breathe; and sunlight to keep warm or generate power. There's also soil, which gives rise to plants with edible fruit/vegetables plus medicinal value while providing defense from bad weather.

Animals offer sustenance along with fabric material and at times transport. Lastly, minerals become essential ingredients when crafting armaments, but don't forget they're also useful for constructing tools like shovels. In a world decimated by human activity, look to mother nature to provide for you, the planet will provide and adapt one way or another.

Improvised Fallout Shelters

In the wake of a nuclear assault, obtaining shelter can be a matter of life and death if you haven't planned. As government-constructed fallout shelters may not exist or are limited in quantity, individuals must think outside the box and use their resources to construct makeshift refuges for themselves against radiation exposure. FEMA's guidance on fallout paths combined with NukeMap's technology, will aid people in visualizing potential zones where radioactive particles could collect after an explosion.

The techniques used when constructing emergency bombproof dwellings vary based on personal circumstances as well as location. Basements, pre-prepared areas specially designed for security from harmful radiation, and custom-crafted structures using metals like steel or concrete are all feasible alternatives. The average safe depth these hiding places should go is around 10 feet deep. Every individual ought to have nine square feet of room within the structure.

Resourceful utilization of accessible materials coupled with innovative solutions leads to protective coverings being produced that help ward off nuclear fallouts thus saving those looking for safety. Improvised refugee camps offer a very effective defense against residual radioactivity released into our environment due to a harrowing nuclear attack.

If you've gained access or have been invited into someone else's bunker or shelter, remember to be courteous. Offer to help out, or even bring a sealed bottle of wine in to break the ice a bit. A joke can be helpful to leaven the mood of destruction and death, for instance:

Q: Why did Oppenheimer invent the Atomic Bomb?

A: Because he wanted the world to light up.

Do gauge your audience first, that joke may not go down well if anyone is suffering from radiation sickness.

Mental Preparedness

Mental readiness is imperative to manage the strain and uncertainty of a nuclear war. It can help people stay motivated, concentrated, and strong even when facing hardship. In achieving mental preparedness, some useful strategies include deep breathing exercises, practicing mindfulness, building inner strength with a positive attitude, relaxation methods such as talking about issues or mind blocks, arranging an environment conducive to success, and mentally rehearsing everything through visualization techniques. Remaining positive is important, but don't bang on about it too much or people will find you very annoying.

Resilience must also be developed so you can cope with the psychological effects brought on by a nuclear conflict along with its accompanying stressors. Cultivating these two attributes, mental preparedness and resilience is key to surviving during times of global nuclear peril.

In the event of a nuclear attack or war, modern technology can play an important role in increasing one's chances for survival. Personal radiation detectors, smartphone apps, and advanced protective gear are just some of the advancements that have become available to assist.

By utilizing cutting-edge technological tools such as these, it is possible to help mitigate some of the risks associated with potential nuclear exposure and ensure safety during times when extra protection may be required.

Personal Radiation Detectors

Personal radiation detectors can allow you to monitor your environment by detecting and measuring the amount of radiation present. Popular models such as Rad Triage 50, RADTriage Model 50, GQ EMF-390 Meter, D3S wearable personal radiation detector, and EcotestVIP are some examples. With these devices, individuals can detect any hazardous levels of exposure so they may act accordingly with appropriate measures necessary against the danger.

Smartphone Apps

In this day and age of ever-increasing connectivity, smartphones have become a useful tool when it comes to nuclear survival. Programs such as Nuclear War 2, Total City Smash: Nuclear War, Nuclear Submarine inc. Arcade, War Commander: Rogue Assault, and OSM (Offline Survival Manual) offer simulations that serve as vital preparation resources for any eventuality related to atomic warfare.

These apps can help individuals be better prepared in case of an emergency by giving them access to valuable information. This includes advice on how they should react during a nuclear crisis along with checklists about what steps need to be taken before the occurrence.

Protective Gear

Investing in advanced protective gear can greatly enhance an individual's likelihood of surviving a nuclear war. Such items include gas masks, rubber boots, gloves, and anti-radiation clothing like shirts, tank tops, or underwear. Coveralls or rain suits will also offer protection from fallout touching the skin. You should also obtain access to iodide tablets as a precaution against radiation exposure.

The most efficient gear with regards to nuclear survival includes products such as CM-8M gas masks, MIRA Safety Gas Mask, and HAZ-SUITs. These provide additional shielding when facing potentially hazardous conditions caused by atomic warfare. Having access to such equipment could prove lifesaving should they ever be needed due to deadly fallout arising from human-made conflict scenarios.

Community

Although we've already touched on it, the value of community-based approaches to survival can't be emphasized enough. During a nuclear emergency, working together as an entire group will improve the chances of survival for everyone involved greatly. Through collective means such as combining resources and expertise, communities will be capable of forming more effective fallout shelters, passing along precious knowledge or intelligence between one another swiftly, and offering support to all who need it.

Let's go a bit deeper to see how beneficial these tactics really are - from building Neighborhood Fallout Shelters (NFS), to sharing supplies among each other and establishing communication networks within society.

Neighborhood Fallout Shelters

In the event of a nuclear attack, having an emergency plan to ensure family safety is imperative. Building community-based fallout shelters can provide increased protection from these devastating consequences and bring people together in difficult times. Much like the individual shelters discussed throughout this book, more communal structures could take many forms depending on the circumstances. Allowing communities to organize their own refuge facilitates collaboration while potentially increasing chances of survival during this type of crisis.

Sharing Resources

In the event of a nuclear war, it is important to share resources so that everyone has access to basic amenities such as food and shelter. This will not only reduce expended energy when collecting them but also minimize radiation exposure. Collaborating is essential for people's survival. These efforts involve helping one another build fallout shelters, forming communication networks with others, and planning strategies on how best to cope psychologically with living through such an incident.

Communication Networks

The ability to establish communication networks during a nuclear war is essential for the transmission of information and organization of activities. This includes keeping people informed on recent events, designing evacuation plans, as well as providing help to those in need. Communication networks can be set up by way of radio signals, satellites, or cell phone connections.

To ensure effective functioning, there should be one main hub in which the communication centers are. Multiple forms used simultaneously along with an efficient system dedicated only to data sharing are key elements that will bring about successful network connectivity among all citizens involved. This will allow them to stay up to date with newsworthy material while maintaining community stability plus have quick contact if/when needing assistance or to action evacuation procedures.

Sustainable Living

Sustainable living is imperative after a nuclear war as it can reduce the impact of radiation and other destruction caused by such an event. Establishing sustainable practices makes people more resilient in preparing for survival during this period while helping to revive a post-nuclear world afterwards.

Some helpful methods to utilize nature include collecting rainwater, planting crops, and using renewable energy resources. By utilizing sustainability principles individuals are not only able to increase their chances of survival but also contribute greatly to recovery efforts following the conclusion of a nuclear conflict.

CONCLUSION

In this book, we have talked about the immediate actions you must take in the face of a potential incoming nuclear explosion, from identifying early warning signs to seeking out the most effective forms of shelter to increase your odds of surviving the blast itself by protecting yourself against radiation in the fallout.

We have also explored how to survive following the blast, from rationing food and water to dealing with radiation sickness and rebuilding a community, as well as the importance of staying alive and indoors for the first 24 to 72 hours following the blast.

While this information is practical and essential, just remember that no bunker, no amount of canned food, and no iodine tablet can truly ensure that you will survive a nuclear catastrophe - no matter what.

Instead, the key to surviving the aftermath of a nuclear explosion, assuming that you survive the blast itself, will be to be proactive and apply all of the advice collectively that you have learned in this book. Don't just rely on one or two of the tips that we have shared.

Let this book not just be another survival guide that collects dust on your shelf; make it one that you refer back to on an ongoing basis. Remember, preparation and education are vital, but making sure you remember what you have learned so you can apply everything when the time comes is even more so.

Following a nuclear war, adapting to the new environment and living conditions requires having an effective plan in place. Accessing information and having access to devices to monitor radiation levels will help you make informed decisions about safety measures. Gaining community support can be done through groups, volunteering services, or connecting with other survivors who have been affected by the fallout from this nuclear weapon.

No matter how demanding restoring normality after such events may be if met head-on with dedication, agility and preparations, it might just be possible that brighter days will eventually prevail for us all.

Yet just as prevention is best when it comes to radiation exposure, avoiding a nuclear catastrophe in the first place is the ideal scenario. Avoiding any escalation of hostilities that may lead to the use of nuclear weapons, thus creating the kind of destruction described in this book, must be a high priority.

Further, to bring about the eventual elimination of these hazardous arms, take action now by petitioning authorities, joining advocacy organizations dedicated to disarmament, and offering donations toward that cause. This will help reduce any risk associated with nuclear weapons now or later on down the road.

Pray for the best but prepare for the worst.

Made in the USA
Columbia, SC
31 May 2024